TRAVELLING MAN

TRAVELLING MAN

DAVE FOSTER

WORD BOOKS
LONDON

Published by Word Books, London,
a Division of Word (UK) Ltd, Park Lane,
Hemel Hempstead, Hertfordshire, HP2 4TD

ISBN 0 85009 040 7

First published April 1973

ACKNOWLEDGEMENTS:
Quotations from The Living Bible by
permission of Coverdale House Publishers Ltd.

Cover photo: Jean-Luc Ray – C.E.P.A.

Printed in Great Britain by
Hunt Barnard Printing Ltd., Aylesbury, Bucks.

Dedicated to

MY TRAVEL AGENTS

CONTENTS

FOREWORD

by Cliff Richard

There are certain people to whom everything seems to happen, and Dave Foster is one of those people.

When I read this book, I caught myself wondering if all this could really have happened to one man. Then I thought of Dave and realised that there is only one man that all this could possibly have happened to!

Dave in this book says of me, and I quote, 'He is the most placid and panic-free traveller I know'. That is because to me a journey is a journey that simply starts at A and ends at B, with occasional diversions to C because of fog. Invariably everything is *very* normal. But to Dave every customs officer, ticket collector, pilot, steward, etc. etc. is an adventure to be lived through, and I must say that I'm glad to have lived through some of them with him – even though sometimes it was touch and go! Life certainly isn't dull when you're with our 'travelling man' and one thing constantly leaps out of these pages – that life is what you make it.

In his travelling for Eurovangelism, Dave could have spent many hours of total boredom but God has given him an exceptional view of life, enabling him to cope with what would wear many of us away.

Now I wouldn't say that he lives, eats, sleeps airlines . . . but my Christmas present from him was a set of six glasses on which are painted the names and slogans of six airlines. One of them tells me that if I fly with them then I'll 'feel more important'. Another says that if I were flying with them I'd 'be there by now'. I don't know whether to have a drink or book a flight!

One thing is for certain. If qualification for heaven depended on the number of flights we made, Dave would 'be there by now'.

Cliff Richard

INTRODUCTION

This book may be unique in that it was featured by its publishers in a full-scale advertising campaign some months before it was actually written!

This did not so much demonstrate the publisher's faith in my ability to produce a usable manuscript, even before he set eyes on the first page, as it was my inability to meet a deadline.

I take full responsibility! A month set aside to write the book was invaded by all kinds of emergencies from unavoidable crises communicated by a telephone I can never escape, to a full-scale alert from an impacted wisdom tooth which wouldn't wait to be removed. History records that during thirty days set aside to write at my home base in Geneva, I made unexpected trips to Monte Carlo, Prague, Zagreb, London and Belfast. With a full travel schedule the next month, I couldn't possibly get back to the book.

Five months later I realised that being a 'travelling man' is the greatest hindrance to writing a book about it. Newspaper and magazine articles I can dash off on plane flights and in hotel rooms, but writing a book is something else. The battle was finally won in the basement of our Swiss home and at my faithful secretary's trusty typewriter in our British office. To her, Miss Maureen Jones, who has now survived the ordeal of churning out manuscripts for two of my books, goes my sincere appreciation.

Credit must also be given to such literary innovators as

Mary Endersbee, George Hoffman and David Winter who, while cohorts in a now-scattered CRUSADE Magazine team, gave me the basic idea for all this. They commissioned me to do a monthly series under the same title, and I am grateful to CRUSADE's present editor John Capon for permission to use some of that material which forms a fraction of the book you now hold.

In the case of George, who is of course Director of TEAR Fund, this book will undoubtedly cause him to re-live some shared experiences. He is one of my favourite travelling companions, and I will be grateful to him if he refrains from publishing an appendix of stories I haven't told!

Thanks also to Bill Latham, veteran journalist and editor, valued friend and counsellor, who 'looked over' the manuscript for me.

Finally, I must mention my marvellous and now more or less stationary wife who makes the life of this 'travelling man' so bearable by surviving my absences, enhancing my homecomings and accepting the more frustrating loneliness of having me home but shut away with a typewriter working on this book!

With her are two children long accustomed to a father who is often someplace else. Our youngest. Alison, used to try and remember where I was at particular times so she could pray for me. Finally, one night, the business of keeping track became too much and she transferred the burden to broader shoulders as she prayed: 'Lord bless Daddy . . . wherever he is!'

DAVE FOSTER,
Geneva, Switzerland.

Chapter One

ONE DAY IN THE LIFE

The alarm-clock sounds at precisely six o'clock. I thrust out a barely-controlled hand and nearly knock it off the bedside table.

The ringing stops. I glance at my wife. Her eyes open ever-so-slightly. They seem to focus for a split second.

'Happy birthday, darling,' she mumbles before the mists of sub-consciousness submerge her once again.

Birthday! That's right! Her brief utterance is more effective than the alarm-clock in snapping me to total awareness. Today is May 9, 1972, and I am thirty-eight years of age. (Usually I find it difficult to remember my age, but the previous night my ten-year-old daughter Alison reminded me by claiming I would be eighty-three, then correcting it with the apologetic explanation that she 'knew there was an eight in it somewhere'!)

On the way to the bathroom, I glance into the kitchen. There on the table is a card and some gift-wrapped parcels. My curiosity is sufficient to cause a detour.

'Blessings on your happy, grinning face,' is the message on one.

It refers to what happened when I arrived home from a trip two days before. The whole family came to the airport to meet me. Waiting in the car outside, they were craning their necks to see who would be first to spot me. Suddenly, much to the amusement of the rest, my twelve-year-old son Paul exclaimed: 'There's his happy, grinning face!'

The gifts are predictable . . . and acceptable.

'Birthdays aren't so bad,' I think, resuming my trip to the bathroom.

Back in the bedroom I dress quietly so as not to disturb my wife. But why bother? Within moments there is another infernal ringing. This time it's her turn to fumble alongside the bed and silence the offending noise-maker.

Six-thirty. Within half-an-hour the children must be roused. Swiss schools start early. They must be there by seven-fifty-five.

Outside, builders are already working on a nearby site. This morning it's not as bad as in the depth of winter. The sun is already shining brightly and the air pleasantly warm.

Back in the kitchen I raid the refrigerator and find some Israeli orange juice. Bliss! I can't eat at this time in the morning, but sipping cold orange juice and thinking of my favourite country is a pleasant way to start the day.

Alison arrives, sorry that she missed the opening of Daddy's presents (why didn't I think of that and wait?) but pleased to be ahead of her sleepier brother. She greets me only moments before Paul staggers in, much less alert, in fact almost sleep-walking. He collapses into my arms, makes an incredible attempt at singing 'Happy Birthday', mercifully gives up in the middle but mumbles the wish anyway.

A few minutes later it's time to leave. Quick kisses all round and I head for the car. It starts easily and by the time I am driving by the end of the garden the children are wide awake and dashing across the lawn to wave goodbye . . . Alison washed, groomed and immaculately dressed, Paul wearing pyjama trousers, a T-shirt inscribed 'Racing Manager' and a look which betrays his desperate need of a comb, soap and water!

At seven o'clock, Geneva traffic is already heavy enough for me to zig-zag through less cluttered back-streets across town to the airport. When I left home it was past check-in time for my flight, but SWISSAIR's check-in girls are a sympathetic crowd. By the time I dump my car in the parking lot and dash to the departure area, I am grateful for the fact that at this time of the morning the lines are rarely long.

'Vienna today?' asks the girl who takes my ticket, failing to note its continuation back to Geneva.

'No,' I explain, 'that's one of my transit stops on the way home.'

'Oh yes,' she agrees, 'so you're going to Frankfurt on your first flight.'

She gives me my boarding card and I dash through the now-familiar control points of Geneva Airport. I know it so well it is almost like an extension of home!

Strapping myself into the seat of a LUFTHANSA Boeing 737, I glance at my watch. Seven-thirty-five. I wonder if the children are on schedule . . . almost ready to get their bicycles from the garage and leave for school.

We take off into the clear blue Swiss sky. This is a more civilised hour, I think, as the stewardess hands me a breakfast tray. One hour later, I see traffic-clogged autobahns below, just before touching down at Frankfurt's magnificent new airport.

I am still at a disadvantage here. It was opened only two months before and while most major European airports are familiar I have had only three brief stopovers in this one. But once the general procedure of any large airport is understood, it is possible to master the system anywhere. I remember one writer who described an airport terminal building as 'a monstrous machine disguised as a building and designed to process people and baggage. To the machine, there is no difference between men, women, children, suitcases, pets. All are collected, screened according to route, classified by status, divided into units of the right size, packaged in aircraft – and shipped.'

This morning's transit stop is a quick one . . . just long

enough to buy a London daily paper and mail a letter. I signed the letter in my office the previous day, noticed it was addressed to Frankfurt and thought that by mailing it this morning I could save on postage. Such thinking may seem bizarre for someone who seems to be running up a pretty hefty air travel bill for one day. But, in fact. by a too-complicated-to-explain situation, I am not only travelling free today but am actually increasing the value of funds to be used in Christian service! So saving a few pfennigs on a stamp still makes sense.

At nine-fifty the autobahn traffic has thinned out as our plane takes off for its East European destination. I settle down to read my newspaper . . . a sample of free press which will be totally unobtainable where I am to land.

Arriving in Eastern Europe always evokes mixed emotions. Even the most innocent traveller can sometimes become the victim of an unpredictable whim of the authorities. But usually there is nothing to worry about. Being a born optimist I work on the assumption that all will go well anyway, showing suitable surprise if it doesn't. Others approach things from the opposite side and, unfortunately, tend to be the ones who come unstuck.

For instance, the optimist who approaches a belligerent-looking passport control officer with a smile and friendly greeting is likely to have less trouble than the pessimist who shows a diffidence which may be misinterpreted as guilt. The 'belligerence' of the official is probably the result of boredom. If some smiling character comes along and relieves the monotony of his job, the sour look usually goes too! Some of the friendliest passport and Customs officials I have met in the whole world are in Eastern Europe. Maybe that's because there I tend to work harder to crack the thin veneer of officialdom to reveal the real person behind the mask.

At Passport Control, an incoming passenger is being

held back because he has overlooked a particular point of procedure. The official trying to explain this to him is being very patient. I am let through without delay.

Customs officers are having a great time going through the baggage of some American tourists. It looks as if I'll be in line for ages until another Customs officer appears, beckons me to one side and stamps my visa form without so much as asking what is in my bulging suitcase! He waves me through another channel. I've arrived.

Currency exchange lines are a necessary evil which cannot be avoided in Eastern Europe. When going to any part of Western Europe I can obtain local currency in advance, but in Communist countries it is usually illegal to export or import their currency. So, since it is obligatory to change a certain amount for each day of a visitor's stay, everyone is doing it on arrival. The fact that there is only one exchange counter for all incoming passengers can make this simple procedure an endless drag.

Knowing my way around this airport enough to take short-cuts and reach the exchange counter ahead of other passengers on my flight, I am only fifth in what soon becomes a long, snaking line. I shouldn't be long except that the four in front of me are first-time American tourists.

Travelling the airways of Europe, I dread the advent of the tourist season. Most planes have their fair share of American passengers, but off-season these tend to be quiet, efficient and highly-intelligent businessmen. I am sure some of the summer tourists can be described in this way but accuracy compels me to record that there are some who are loud, slow and incredibly stupid. Those ahead of me this morning belong to this category. In spite of the excellent English of the girl behind the counter, they seem totally incapable of understanding the simplest instructions like, 'Please sign your travellers' cheques'.

The first couple finally complete their transaction with the man swearing he's been fiddled and the woman claiming loudly that the local currency 'looks like kids' money'. Next in line are two ageing matrons wearing metallic-coloured wigs which look like wire wool. They face a crisis of a different kind; one has lost her visa form. I give myself a half-hearted reprimand for being ungracious enough to be pleased at this development. She is still searching through all kinds of hand-baggage while I complete my currency exchange in thirty seconds flat?

The man who meets me is one of my favourite people. He is engaged in Christian service carried on under the toughest of conditions. We wait until we are in the car to say more than a few words of greeting. The expression 'walls have ears' may have originated in Eastern Europe. But a car is a 'safe' place to talk, and an excellent place to pray.

'Dear Lord,' he prays, 'only you know how much it means for us to have dear brother Dave here again. We thank you for all those in the West who love you and love us . . . and for the way they express this love through our dear brother.'

He goes on to thank God for difficulties 'because through them we prove your power.'

Soon we're heading for town. It's near enough to May Day for red flags to be flying everywhere. The sun is shining and the flags encourage a festive atmosphere which is in stark contrast to all I hear of the latest situation here.

Reaching his home, we greet his wife . . . and pray again. This man seems so addicted to prayer that if he doesn't indulge in it every couple of hours he begins to feel uneasy!

Lunch is an event! The fine spread is not characteristic of the way they usually eat. Everything is special, even to the birthday cake dessert!

The real business of the visit follows. Intense discussion. Note-taking. Suggestions. Promises of prayerful assistance. Quick decisions when necessary. Commitments by faith. And, inevitably, more prayer.

All too quickly, it is time to go. A late afternoon drive to the airport is followed by reluctant farewells. I wander into the departure area alone. It is time for me to check in for my flight out, but I delay this deliberately. I am not feeling like being subjected to spot checks and interrogation, so purposely I dash through late. They know my flight is due to leave soon and, unless I am under suspicion they are not likely to make me miss it.

The official checking me out of the country has just finished exhaustive questioning of the previous passenger, to whom he spoke in English.

I smile and greet him in his own language. Then add, 'I'm amazed at how well you speak English!'

He smiles, and replies modestly: 'I make many mistakes.'

'If I could speak your language with as few mistakes, I'd be happy,' I tell him sincerely.

He grins again, stamps my papers and says: 'Have a good flight.'

I find Vienna Airport uninspiring. Today I reach it tired, which doesn't help. The fact that my ongoing flight to Zurich is delayed isn't encouraging either. Fortunately there is not a tight connection with my Geneva flight so I am not too concerned. I find a quiet corner to sit and write notes.

We are only forty-five minutes late arriving in Zurich. Still in time for the last flight of the day to Geneva. And with sufficient transit time for me to put through a call to my wife and let her know I am back in Switzerland.

We chat for two francs and twenty centimes worth of time, swapping stories about the day's happenings like any married couple. She says the children behaved themselves. I say the Secret Police have been enquiring into my activities but are not mad at me. She says she has been shopping this afternoon. I remark that the shops where I was were closed. She says she is very tired although she hasn't done all she planned. I remind her I drove myself to the airport and that she doesn't have to come and meet me, so why doesn't she go to bed.

My flight is called ahead of time to allow for the stringent personal security checks the Swiss still rigidly maintain. After fumbling through my baggage and feeling over my person, the friendly uniformed officer lets me through to board my final flight of the day – a huge DC8 going to Geneva, Rio, Sao Paulo, Buenos Aires and Santiago. I am glad to be getting off at the first stop, thirty minutes after departure.

The only curious thing I notice on this short, uneventful hop is the illuminated 'Seat Belt' signs. In Economy Class, where I am sitting, the sign says FASTEN SEAT BELTS. But I can see through to the First Class section where a similar illuminated request is preceded by PLEASE. I wonder if it was intentional on the part of a designer and whether he harboured a weird idea that politeness increases with affluence!

Geneva's night air is cooler than that of early morning. As I walk to where I parked my car more than sixteen hours before, I marvel again at the potential of jet travel. Not all my trips to Eastern Europe are as fast, but few could have been more significant.

Unlocking the door of my darkened home, I creep into the bedroom where my wife is already tucked snugly in bed. Her eyes open ever-so-slightly. They seem to focus for a split second.

'Hello darling,' she mumbles before the mists of subconsciousness submerge her again. 'Have a good day?'

'Very good, thanks love,' I reply, loosening my tie. 'And you?'

'Goodnight darling,' she says, almost in her sleep and not hearing my question.

'Goodnight darling,' I whisper, kissing her forehead.

She is already asleep.

Chapter Two

GETTING STARTED

Until the age of eighteen, I was a most unlikely candidate for the title of 'travelling man'. Born in the West of England, my childhood was spent in a home from which we rarely moved far. My parents – no great travellers – still live there. From this isolated South Devonshire vantage point even London seemed about as accessible as the back side of the moon. My first trip there included such memorable experiences as viewing television for the first time.

My mother was so concerned about her then only son that on my first major pre-teen train trip, all of 38 miles to my grandparents' home in Cornwall, I was consigned to riding with the Guard who happened to be a friend of the family. My parents didn't own a car, so motoring was a rare pleasure to be enjoyed only on odd occasions. I did ride the double-deck bus four miles to the nearest city, Plymouth. But I rarely managed the trip without succumbing to travel sickness!

My first enjoyable means of transportation was a bicycle. And, on one historic day, I actually pedalled my way to St Austell, home of my grandparents. My mother's apprehension soared to dizzy heights. But the successful accomplishment of such a feat in a fairly static family was greeted with the kind of acclaim reserved for an Olympic gold medallist.

Feet pumping and pedals flashing through the Cornish countryside, I was on my way to a life which was to be characterised by almost constant motion!

Becoming a Christian at the age of fifteen probably set the seal on it. Those whose lives attracted me to making this commitment were in the organisation known as 'Youth for Christ'. While those in the local group were as bound in their geographical limitations as I was, the movement encouraged a world vision. Such great-sounding slogans as 'The Evangelisation of the World in our Generation' were tossed around. Young American evangelists in pale drape suits and screamingly loud ties 'flew in' for meetings. They talked about crossing the Atlantic with the nonchalance of crossing a street. It was soon impressed on me that if I was to be a part of evangelising the world I'd have to think in broader terms than cycling to St Austell!

Military service was my real point of emancipation from the myopia of West country ruralism. I flew for the first time. I lived away from home. I could test the validity of my Christian experience outside the protective wrappings of evangelical tradition. And then I was posted to Pakistan.

My world view broadened. Second-hand accounts of 'the mission field' became first-hand experiences. Recognition of that which was once so remote now hit me with startling clarity.

One night, after a delightful meal in one of Karachi's top restaurants, I had difficulty in getting a taxi. A short walk in the warm, night air to where I knew I would find one appealed to me. And anyway, it would help me dispel the discomfort of an overfilled stomach.

Previous exploration of the city had always been during the day, but as I walked in the late evening a startingly different night scene unfolded. Streets were filled with destitute people sleeping in doorways, gutters and even on traffic islands. I stopped and stared, suddenly feeling so incongruous, even ridiculous, in my white tuxedo.

No one seems to care, I thought. Others making for the

taxi rank seemed oblivious to the sad-looking sea of subconscious humanity around. They'd probably seen it all before . . . enough times to be buffered by familiarity. But, for me, the first shock of the immense poverty of these people did much to develop my thinking about Christian responsibility.

Beneath the bright tropical moon, I stood on a deserted street corner and prayed: 'Lord, never let me be insensitive to human need. Make me ready to go whereever that need is great.'

Feelings at that point were rather vague. It wasn't a very profound prayer. I was already a Christian with a 'sound evangelical' background. My evangelistic zeal was probably above average. This was born in my early contact with 'Youth for Christ' and nurtured by a natural inclination to being something of an extrovert. But somehow, until tonight, I had tended to think of 'souls' rather than 'people'. The criterion of my concern was related almost exclusively to a spiritual dimension not recognised by the average person. Suddenly I saw how futile it would be to wake up one of those sleeping beggars and say: 'Friend, are you saved?' It would have been more appropriate to give him my tuxedo to supplement his inadequate rags and take him back to the restaurant where I had just stuffed myself with enough food to last him a month!

Back in Britain, evangelism was hitting the front pages of national dailies for the first time in living memory. Billy Graham, whose first itinerant ministry was in the razzmatazz of the movement which meant so much to me, was blazing an unbelievable trail of traditional evangelism in London's Harringay Arena. Sheaves of press clippings came through the mail daily and I ached to be there rather than being stuck with what seemed the rather futile responsibility of controlling air traffic half a world away.

Knowing what God was doing in London and seeing

what Christians should be doing in Karachi balanced my thinking about evangelism and social action. In common with many other Christians, I had seen my responsibility simply in terms of holding meetings and preaching sermons (as well as 'personal work' which amounted to doing the same thing singly). Missionary work was a variation of this where candidates were recruited to be sent overseas to hold meetings and preach sermons. Of course, I knew that some missionaries did medical work, but I considered the prime purpose of such 'peripheral' activity was keeping a toe in an otherwise closing door or providing a means to con sick people into conversion.

Now I began to view things differently. My thinking developed rather than adjusted. Then, as now, I still placed a priority on the need for Christian conversion. I refused to relegate 'the preaching of the Word' to any place less than the high position God gives it. Interchange of personnel for missionary service is and always will be important, even if the character of the task changes to adjust to new situations. But I saw that Paul, for example, did not confine himself solely to standing in the pulpit. In Acts 11: 29 & 30 (L.B) a great famine is forecast, 'So the believers decided to send relief to the Christians in Judea, each giving as much as he could. This they did, consigning their gifts to Barnabas and Paul to take to the elders of the church in Jerusalem.'

Since then I have learned to articulate my feelings along these lines far better, but never as succinctly and effectively as I heard it from my friend Bill Latham. Now working with TEAR Fund, Bill was once a schoolteacher. During eight years in this profession he became used to answering children's questions. But one struck him with such force that he's still challenged by it. The boy asked, very simply: 'What do Christians *do*?' Which caused Bill to conclude that if people see Christians *doing* things in society, then there will be a much greater response to our gospel message.

Such thoughts crowded my mind after that unforgettable experience in the middle of Karachi. But on my return to Britain, God had an unexpected plan of 'apprenticeship' lined up for me.

Chapter Three

WHITE CAR WITH RED SEATS

The rain was coming down in sheets across a coal-encrusted valley somewhere north of Cardiff. From the front room of a tiny terraced house, I viewed the dismal scene with a sense of foreboding. Soon I would be forced to leave the warm hospitality of this little Welsh home and face the elements as I crossed the valley to my next meeting.

In those early days as an itinerant evangelist, I spent most of my time showing Christian films. This gave me the advantage of not having to prepare too many sermons! But with it was the distinct disadvantage of having more than a Bible and toothbrush to haul around with me. In fact I was continually lumbered with a projector, amplifier, accessories case, some 16 mm films and a six-foot screen. All this, and no car. The fact that I never slipped a disc nor suffered a heart attack while hustling porters to get me aboard trains (which always left slap on time whenever I chose to travel in them) can only be explained by the fact that I had youth on my side.

But no trains ran across this rain-drenched valley. Buses were out. (Well, have you ever tried negotiating a six-foot screen aboard a single-decker?) No one involved in my meetings appeared to possess a car, but the organiser assured me that somehow he would arrange to transport me from A to B. Counting on this, I didn't call a taxi . . . or rather, *the* taxi.

Suddenly, out of the gathering gloom, my transportation trundled up. It was a sad-looking horse pulling an open cart! I was horrified. Did they expect me to travel on that wearing my only decent suit . . . exposed to the elements . . . and with my precious equipment getting soaked as it bumped along roads disfigured by the subsidence of mines deep below?

'I'll take the taxi,' I suggested.

'Misuse of the Lord's money,' muttered the man who had brought the cart.

'But the equipment will be damaged,' I pleaded, refraining from stating the obvious that I would get soaked as well.

'They travelled this way in the Welsh Revival,' came the reply.

'But Evan Roberts didn't have fragile and expensive equipment,' I protested.

Happily, the horse did not appear to be taking sides.

Finally, in a desperate effort to convince, I telephoned to check if my insurance company would take the risk of the equipment travelling in this way. I was told that the policy covered only 'normal means of transportation' and whether this included a horse and cart was highly questionable.

That settled it. I called the taxi.

The incident came to mind many years later when we were travelling to a remote part of Yugoslavia. This time we had musical instruments which refused to fit with five people into the Fiat 600 which met us at the railway station. Speaking no Serbo-Croatian, there was no possibility of joining the excited discussion which ensued. Finally the problem was solved as the jubilant Yugoslavs explained that while we travelled a circuituous route by car, the instruments would be conveyed along a shorter route . . . by horse and cart.

This time I didn't protest. At least it wasn't raining, and I wasn't about to make an international telephone call to the insurance company. So, with the assurance that the instruments would recline gently on a bed of soft straw, we paid the man with the horse and cart and said we would see him at the church.

Three hours later, we were still waiting for him! Our car journey was comparatively short, and we had eaten a meal expecting to hear the cart arriving at any moment. But nothing happened, and now it was getting near the time of the meeting. The church was packed, but our group couldn't get started without the instruments.

Dark thoughts about his honesty were dispelled when, at the last moment, the man with the horse and cart rolled into town . . . roaring drunk! The instruments were fine, but the reason for his delay was obvious.

During long years of constant travel in the cause of Christian service, I have learned many things. Two of them are to avoid horses and carts as a mode of travel whenever possible and, if such transportation is unavoidable, pay the driver *after* he has delivered the goods!

Much travelled comedian Bob Hope once commented on his comings and goings: 'Somewhere high in my family tree, I must have had a relative who was a mule-skinner for Marco Polo, or a gypsy dancer, or a railway attendant – or maybe it's because my mother put jet fuel in my milk.'

I've always been too busy travelling to examine my family tree, but as one who shares the worldwide commission given to those much-travelled members of the Early Church I must admit that I do not dislike my 'journeyings often'. This never ceases to amaze me when I remember that, as a child, I couldn't survive that four-mile bus ride without being travel sick.

Some claim that travel sickness is a psychological affliction. There may be grounds for this, because I didn't just grow out of it. Even now I watch the weather forecast with special interest whenever I am due to cross the Channel . . . in fact sea travel is the only form of transportation which still causes me concern in this way.

The reason I think there is a psychological aspect to it stems from one of my first overnight voyages across the North Sea. The weather couldn't have been worse. While having a bath before going to bed, I kept both taps turned full on the entire time. No sooner had the tub half-filled than the ship would give a mighty heave and send my carefully accumulated bath-water cascading across the bathroom. Fortunately the drainage grills in the floor were capable of coping.

The fact that I was sharing a cabin with a veteran and much-travelled missionary made me determine that I'd do my level best to ride the waves as well as him without turning green. All night long the boat heaved and rolled its way across the North Sea, and the dawn brought no respite from the howling gale. I staggered out of my bunk, somewhat dizzy but still remarkably strong of stomach. As I was getting dressed the prostrate form of the globe-trotting man of God moved slightly.

'Where are you going?' he asked.

'To breakfast,' I replied. Coming?'

'Ugh-h-h-h!' he groaned, and disappeared beneath the blankets.

Months later, having acquired a wife to share my cabin, we were travelling across the Atlantic on one of the world's largest and most modern liners. But the fact that the ship's kitchens produced the most fantastic culinary creations imaginable was lost to us for the first four days. We were both sea-sick until the final day when, white and wasted, we forced ourselves to face food. Assigned to the same table was a man who did justice to the full menu while we picked sullenly at dishes fit for a king.

'Travel by sea much?' I asked, not really interested but feeling that polite conversation might stimulate my mind enough to get it off my stomach.

'This is my forty-first Atlantic crossing!' he said jubilantly, still tucking into his fifth course.

'Never considered flying?' I ventured.

'What?' he asked, 'And miss five days of this glorious food?'

'It's our first sea crossing,' I admitted.

I didn't add that even then I was determined it would be our last. The first two things we did on arrival in New York were to claim a refund on our return boat tickets and book a flight with PAN AMERICAN.

Years have passed, and the child my wife was expecting when we flew back to London is now a teenager. Together with his younger sister, he is accustomed to seeing me pack my case, and asking: 'Where to this time, Dad?'

Leaving the family is never easy, particularly when it means handing my wife the responsibility of coping with two children. But both of them have made it easier by never showing undue resentment over my absences. In fact. Paul's most memorable answer to prayer was related to my travels.

After moving our home to Switzerland (we have had this central European base for ten years now) we were without a car. A friend kindly loaned us a vehicle for an extended period but, as that had to be returned, we were back to Square One again.

Our then little boy was just beginning to understand one aspect of prayer. To him it was, basically, ask and receive.

'If we ask God for a car, He'll send us one, won't He?' he asked with childish simplicity, one night.

'Well . . . er . . . yes,' I replied, trying not to sound too dubious, and therefore lacking in faith.

'Well let's ask then,' he concluded, dropping to his knees alongside his bed.

I joined him as he began not only to pray for a car, but to stipulate the colour of bodywork, upholstery and, for good measure, one or two accessories! I was horrified, but restrained myself from stifling his simple faith by suggesting that *maybe* God wouldn't send us *just* the car *we* thought we needed, etc., etc.

More mature prayers, but certainly with no greater faith, were offered later by my wife and me when our son was sleeping. The same evening the telephone rang heralding the fastest answer to a prayer of this kind we ever experienced – before or since!

On the line was a couple concerned about the transportation they were sure we needed. By the time the conversation concluded, they had committed themselves to investing in our ministry to the extent of the full price of a brand new car! It was more than I dared hope for, but perhaps the first thought that struck me was that I would be able to *choose* the colour. There was no question of deciding this because Paul had already stipulated a white car with red seats – and that's what I ordered from the Ford factory in Germany.

I was going by train to Cologne to pick up the new car, and it was my wife who made the unusual suggestion that I take Paul with me. He was thrilled . . . and the climax of his adventure was when there in front of the showroom he came face-to-radiator with the car he had prayed for.

With his travelling father, he climbed into this new means of transportation. We bowed our heads together, thanked God for His provision and drove off toward Switzerland in our white car with red seats.

Chapter Four

TRAVELLING MAN JUNIOR

Airlines try to increase ticket sales by convincing executives that travelling is enhanced by taking their wives with them. A few years after I started travelling, I acquired a wife who came with me frequently during our first years of marriage.

Even our wedding was tied in to my travels and took place at the end of a Youth Congress in Copenhagen, Denmark. Whenever someone hears where I was married, the next question is inevitably: 'Is your wife Danish?' She isn't, but this was the only place we could get together the American clergyman who conducted the ceremony, the South Africans who played the organ and sang, my British best man and the Canadian who took the pictures. They were all travelling men!

Susan began to travel with me. In 1958, the first year after our marriage, we visited almost every county of England, Scotland and Wales. In the same year, I fitted in trips to five other countries but, when I went overseas I usually left my wife at home. That was until an incident in October of that year.

I was preparing for a trip to Spain while Sue was resigning herself to a lonely month at home in Eastbourne. If she was to come with me, we would be personally responsible for her expenses and we couldn't afford it. But just before I left, the colleague who was to accompany me had to cancel out. His ticket was going begging. That night we prayed about it, and the following morning someone with no knowledge of the situation sent us a gift of *the exact amount necessary to buy the ticket*!

That month we stepped up a fast-developing sideline of writing for the Christian press by launching a weekly youth page in the now-defunct SUNDAY COMPANION. It seems funny now that someone described it as 'the most up-to-date and helpful feature in weekly religious journalism' because most of it was churned out on the move. Weekly deadlines demanded discipline. Often I was writing way into the night before press day. Sometimes the page was costing the paper plenty when much of it was dictated by long distance telephone. Frequently it would run up additional compositor's costs when we missed a deadline and filed 'late copy'.

Susan stood the pressures and complications of constant travel well, even when someone stole her suitcase on Euston Station. We were returning from a month of travel and she had been carrying just about all of the few clothes she possessed.

By the beginning of 1959 we were told to expect the addition of a tiny traveller to make us a trio. Sue's last trip before motherhood was to the United States. We flew back from New York the middle of August; Paul was born before the middle of September. When he arrived, we recorded all our happy thoughts in a letter to him, to be kept until he was old enough to understand it. This began: 'When you get a little older, Paul, we will recount to you the circumstances that caused you to be a much-travelled baby even before you were born! Before that warm September morning when you finally made your debut, you already covered many thousands of miles by car, train, boat and plane. If that's the Lord's way of setting the pace for your life, we have no doubt you'll be a world traveller!'

A month after he was born, his mother made a diary note: 'Paul is already on the move almost as much as his father. In the first three weeks of his life he stayed in three different homes, finally arriving at No. 4 which happened to be his own.' The next month he and his mother joined me at an evangelistic crusade I was conducting in Essex. After returning home briefly, we all travelled to Plymouth for Christmas.

Again Sue noted: 'The only thing limiting the radius of Paul's travels is the fact that he does not yet have a passport!'

By the time Susan was expecting our second baby she decided it was time to hang up her travelling clothes and settle to the life of a more normal housewife, homemaker and mother.

At first I hated the thought of returning to lone travel again, especially now I was a father, but we all knew it had to be. For Sue to continue travelling would be unfair to the children, and she had experienced enough of living out of suitcases to look forward to a more settled existence.

By now we had moved into a house and, for the first time, my wife placed a regular order for a daily newspaper. That simple action proved to me she was serious about staying home!

Chapter Five

SANCTIFIED JET-SETTER

Travel was once just a matter of going and coming, but now it can be a whole way of life. Some businessmen spend more time in planes than at office desks. TV personalities, such as David Frost, commute across the Atlantic regularly. Even the average once-a-year holiday-maker seems to be venturing farther and farther for his vacation.

At its best, travel enriches human experience. At its worst, it involves traffic jams, pollution and, for those who take to the air, what one veteran of the skies describes gloomily as 'the propulsion of a sealed capsule through featureless space'.

At one time airlines were simply conveyors of passengers, but now they involve themselves in everything from hotel reservations to package holidays, from car rentals to entertainment. Competition is keen and, while the International Air Transport Association keeps its members within common fare structures, airline advertising must find something special, even unique, to attract the customer.

For the Christian, concerned about the completion of the Great Commission to 'go . . . into all the world, and preach the gospel to every creature', the proliferation of modern travel should seem like a God-given tool to finish an otherwise 'impossible' task. But, in point of fact, there are still those who, while not batting an eyelid at the commendable operation of airlifting life-saving drugs to a disaster area, ask all kinds of questions when a servant of God multiplies the scope of his ministry by purchasing a plane ticket!

Happily we are progressing beyond the point where Billy Graham once arrived in London, having crossed the Atlantic in 'unseemly' luxury, to be reminded that 'Jesus came to Jerusalem riding on a donkey'. The spontaneous response of one of his colleagues must be a classic in the Graham archives: 'If you can find a donkey that can swim the Atlantic, we'll get Billy to ride him!'

As well as the surprising number of Christians who shun air travel, there are still a few who actually condemn it, an admittedly small minority who still trot out the old chestnut, 'If God meant us to fly, He would have given us wings!' (The reply to that being that although we didn't get wings, He did give us the laws of aerodynamics.)

Radio was once condemned as 'of the Devil'. Some further elaborated on this by explaining that Satan is the 'prince of the power of the air'. But today, radio is recognised as a potent means of propagating the gospel, especially as it penetrates areas where the freedom of full religious expression is denied. Television suffered similarly, but has proved itself an equally powerful and perhaps more persuasive medium of Christian communication.

People sometimes assume that a man who travels constantly must be a restless soul who is either dissatisfied with his home, can't stand his wife, has a poor relationship with his children . . . or all three! In some cases this may be true, but not in mine. I enjoy my home which is beautifully kept by a charming wife and shared by two loving children and a dog. My natural inclination is to stay there, but a greater compulsion keeps me travelling. One thing I have discovered about my time spent at home is that while the *quantity* of it may be less than many husbands and fathers, the *quality* is enhanced because we really treasure every moment together.

Another widely-held misconception is that travel is a chore. This may be true for some, but usually only until it becomes so frequent as to be second nature. Packing is often a problem to those who do it little more than once a year, but for someone who faces it many times a month the average suitcase can be filled inside five minutes with no essential item omitted.

An airport can be a formidable place to someone who seldom flies, its formalities complicated and baffling. But whereas my local airport holds no mystery for me, catching a bus across town is something to be avoided at all costs! Our conductor-less buses now force the intrepid traveller to master the intricacies of a ticket machine before beginning his journey. This only accepts certain coins which I never seem to have when I need them. By the time I scrounge the correct change and manage to extract the right ticket, the bus has gone!

Is travel tiring? Generally yes, but although I get tired travelling, I never get tired *of* travelling. On the other hand I am not a compulsive traveller bitten by a mobility bug which makes me uneasy spending long in one place. And, in view of the fact that I love my family, enjoy being with them and have a lawn which needs regular attention, I try to control it. I ask myself two questions about every trip. First, is it really necessary? Secondly, how can I complete it in the fastest possible time?

The answer to the second question often causes the average observer to look askance. For one person who heard I achieved the unlikely record of visiting five separate European capitals in the course of a single day, this was all that stuck in her mind whenever my name was mentioned. It wasn't until much later, when she realised there was definite purpose in these seemingly mad manouverings that she assessed me as anything more than some kind of sanctified jet-setter!

Air travel is a great time saver. Apart from the obvious

advantages of getting to a destination in the fastest possible time, a plane is one of the few places where I can be completely free from such sometimes irritating necessities as telephones. During flights I can often accomplish a great deal of work. I write and, if the plane is half empty and it is possible to isolate myself reasonably well, I can dictate into a portable recorder. When nothing else is possible, I catch up on my reading.

Soon after Susan settled at home, I found myself going to the Continent more and more. Mostly this was simply an extension of evangelistic activity at home. I had developed a visual means of presenting the Christian message which overcame language barriers and enjoyed a general popularity. This opened for me doors which otherwise remained closed to Christian communicators. In one European country, a delighted television producer, with more zeal than knowledge in the English language, proudly proclaimed: 'You are zee very first of your species to appear on our national televeesion!'

Looking back over recorded impressions and reports of those days in the early sixties is heartwarming to say the least. One tour report of Portugal includes the following: 'SETUBAL: Every meeting packed, extra seats filled, people standing. Final night crowds overflowed into road outside. Many saw and heard proceedings by climbing up to windows; PORTIMAO: Even larger crowds. People walked more than ten miles to attend one meeting. Final night saw 500 in a church where the average congregation is 80; EVORA: Meetings packed with many standing. Sunday night meeting was chief topic of conversation in High School on Monday morning; PORTO: Many hundreds of people attended three special rallies; LISBON: Packed halls with crowds of up to 1,200 during one week of meetings. Final rally absolutely full with overflow crowds outside.'

Being a temporary widow during such times was eased for Susan when she read reports such as one from our organiser and interpreter in Portugal at this time: '*We praise God for what He has been doing through this special effort. There has been an unusually high percentage of youth attending the meetings. For many of them, this has been their first contact with the Gospel. The encouraging number of definite decisions for Christ does not indicate the full extent of the spiritual results. Many who have heard the Gospel for the first time are now considering its implications and will undoubtedly respond during subsequent contacts.*'

Travel miles mounted, and I can almost relive my own utter weariness when I wrote in May 1961: 'Going to Germany at the end of the long winter season of intensive evangelism was rather like the sprint at the end of a long distance race. But although tired before starting, the Lord gave the extra resources of energy needed to preach nearly 40 times in 21 consecutive days.'

The rest of that year I visited Spain, Switzerland, France, Holland, Belgium and Germany once again. As I came home for Christmas, more tired than I could ever remember, I took heart in something written by another travelling man, as paraphrased by J. B. Phillips in 2 Corinthians, 4:16,17: 'This is the reason we never collapse. The outward man does indeed suffer wear and tear, but every day the inward man receives fresh strength.'

Chapter Six

EUROVANGELISM EMERGES

Switzerland is a good country for any European travelling man to settle. The Swiss, who are trying desperately to control if not curtail the influx of foreigners, will not thank me for that sincere compliment! I understand their feeling that if they've got a good thing they don't want to spoil it.

When I return from crisis areas to this idyllic little land, its spectacular scenery and quiet serenity make it seem like Heaven on earth. I can think of no more happy setting than to be stretched out in the lush grass of a meadow high on the side of a Swiss mountain, the almost uncanny silence broken only by the gentle sound of distant cowbells coming through the clear air.

But that's not what brought us to Switzerland!

One day in 1962, I made a startling discovery. I was spending more time on the Continent than in Britain. Since my wife and two children were in Eastbourne, they were seeing less and less of me. And, since Britain is alongside one corner of the Continental land mass, I felt far removed from them if I was in one of the other corners. The thought did cross my mind that to set up home in central Europe may help overcome this situation.

At about that time I was invited to establish a European office for YFC in Geneva. Suddenly many other things fell into place and, in May 1963, we left our semi-detached security in Britain and set off south rather like Abraham who 'went out not knowing whither'.

For six months, it was back to the suitcases again. I travelled very little during that time, but that's the period it took to find a home of our own. Finally it appeared in the form of a fifth-floor apartment. A new base was established.

Switzerland has proved to be ideal in this way. For someone travelling all over Europe, East and West, it is central. There is no strip of Channel to separate from other countries, so a trans-Continental car journey is not begun with a costly ferry-crossing. Strikes, which can affect a constant traveller in many ways, are unheard of here. The centrality of the situation means I can be home more often, and never as far away when I'm travelling. And, in the course of a year, there is considerable saving in travel expenses. These and many other advantages have kept us here long after the YFC assignment ended.

First journeys from Switzerland were by car and, with two pre-school children, it was often possible for the family to travel too. After running around the Continent with me in 1964, our then four-year-old son asked: 'Daddy, where *do* we live?' When his younger sister piped up: 'In a car!' we decided that it may be best for them to get settled at home before starting school.

Even then their travel experiences reflected in everything. While other children played cowboys, they played Customs officers!

Between mid-January and May the following year, I was home for a total of one week. By the end of that year, I looked back on statistics such as 25,000 miles . . . 10 countries . . . almost 200 major meetings and about 100 newspaper and magazine articles written and published.

At that point, I was ready to quit being a travelling man! Certainly I felt the necessity of taking stock. Was the future to be a continuing merry-go-round of multilingual meetings with 'super-evangelist' Foster flitting across the face of the Continent like a flea in a fit? Or did God have some other plan? Was He trying to say something to us by the fact that after promising to supply our material needs, and never failing, we hit a patch where for three solid months we received no personal income whatever? It wasn't until the day Susan announced that her next trip to the supermarket for essential foodstuffs would have to be cancelled if something didn't happen soon, that the tide turned.

Actually God was already laying the foundations for a new course in the future, but I had been too busy to notice it. As far back as four years before, people started sending money which was not for our ministry. It happened when they would read one of my magazine articles about the work of a European national such as a Portuguese pastor who, with much faith and little finance, began a rescue work for neglected children.

Whenever such gifts came, and they seemed to be increasing in size and frequency, we would pass them on and forget about it. But then, when I stopped to consider, it dawned on my travel-torn thinking processes that this was setting a pattern to be encouraged.

The Apostle Paul, being a travelling man, has always intrigued me. Suddenly a new aspect of this great evangelist came into sharp focus. Alongside his own ministry he made an interesting point of encouraging others, like Timothy. When the records are revealed, this may well be seen as his greatest contribution to the growth of the early Church.

Reviewing my own situation, I saw myself rushing around many language areas without a hope of really mastering anything other than my mother tongue. It's true I could choose to confine myself to one place, immerse myself in a single language and adapt to one particular culture. Missionaries have been doing this for ages but, unless they are among the comparatively few capable of totally saturating themselves in the new scene, they continue to be regarded as foreigners. That's why wise missionaries have, and still do, encouraged and developed national leadership.

Europe is different to developing areas. There are established churches and long religious traditions. Some are strangled by dead ritualism, but in most places there is a faithful minority doing an effective work for God. The problem is that many of these nationals, like my Portuguese friend, are isolated in their own areas and can expect little outside help. The gifts I was able to pass on were the exception rather than the rule.

Suddenly I saw it! If we could find such nationals in whose ministry we could invest, their potential could be used to fulfil even broader visions. It wasn't long before the missionary service organisation known as EURO-VANGELISM was born.

By the end of that year of 1966 it seemed my travels had increased rather than lessened. Our Christmas newsletter recorded: 'This year has taken me from our Swiss home base to Austria, Czechoslovakia, Denmark, England, Finland, France, Germany, Holland, Ireland, Italy, Monaco, Norway, Spain and Sweden. Most of those countries were visited more than once. Czechoslovakia, five times.'

What was accomplished in all this? Records show: 'Our Geneva office has been the administrative hub of significant projects across the entire Continent. Supplying Bibles. Publishing Christian literature. Producing and sponsoring radio broadcasts to Eastern Europe. Encouraging leadership training. Helping to rescue abandoned children. Providing medical help to the poor and underprivileged . . . and much else.'

This new development changed the pattern of my travel. Today its extent is the same, if not greater, but the duration of trips is less. No longer are there month-long marathons. Frequently I will visit a country for a single day.

On one of my typical day trips to another European country, I made notes on what the brief visit accomplished. While there we finalised purchase and details of distribution of hundreds of Bibles, reviewed reception of a recently-published Christian book. Funds for a building project were cleared through official channels. I left enough money to buy another car for evangelistic work there. Manuscripts for a modern paraphrase of the New Testament Gospels were picked up. Relief funds to be dispensed through Christian agencies were dropped off. A brief meeting with Christian leaders to discuss their involvement in an international conference on evangelism. Some cassette recorders were purchased to be used in Christian service. Problems tackled and solved ranged from where to find gold to edge Bibles we were binding, to arranging importation of heavy machinery for a building project.

A friend who accompanied me on one of these trips said: 'I always thought that when you went somewhere, you had most of the day to yourself until the evening meeting!'

Most days there is no evening meeting. By the time one would normally be held, I may be catching up on the food I didn't have time to eat during the day while flying the last plane home!

I must admit that sleeping in my own bed more often is a privilege I appreciate and enjoy. And I don't exactly yearn for the days when I would sleep on a beach or under a hedge because I couldn't afford even the cheapest hotel room. And hitch-hiking was a form of travel I always hated!

Chapter Seven

THE GYPSIES

The cheapest form of travel is hitch-hiking. The most economical accommodation is a tent. Neither appeal to me. But, at times, circumstances forced both.

The most memorable hitching episode began in a Middle Eastern country skirting the Mediterranean and wound up in Iraq. It was many years ago.

The charter plane on which I was travelling put down at a very remote airfield surrounded by desert. Later, when due to leave, it was discovered to be unserviceable. There was no hope of repairing it in such an out-of-the-way place, and little possibility of finding another plane to which to transfer. This was the prelude to the longest and most frustrating stopover I ever experienced.

One week later I was still in the same area trying to solve the problem now complicated by rising tension and military sabre-rattling in the area. It wasn't actual war, but the situation was such a hairsbreadth away from open conflict that I had a keen desire to go to anyplace else on earth. Already I had moved about twenty miles from the airport because the place was a centre of military activity. I arranged with a friendly official to let me know when a plane was leaving on which I might stand the chance of a seat.

Finally his phone call came. There was a remote chance that I may be able to get a seat on a plane leaving in two hours. It was worth a try. The problem was that I had no means of transportation to the airport. Twenty miles of desert road separated me from the possibility of escape, but there were no buses or taxis. Desperately I dragged my baggage out into the middle of the road and flagged down a passing military vehicle. The driver asked me where I was going, and my heart sank as he said he was heading in quite another direction. There was no hope of another vehicle coming along that deserted track.

'Why are you going there?' the driver asked.

'There's a good possibility that I can catch a plane out of here if I get there within the next hour,' I explained.

'If there's a chance of anyone getting out of this – hole,' exclaimed the soldier, 'I'm going to help him! Climb aboard.'

Going completely out of his way, he got me to the airport in time to catch the plane. It happened to be going to Iraq, but I was past caring as I stared happily out of the plane window at the fast-receding desert below.

My only recollection of hitch-hiking in Europe followed an unfortunate car accident. Late one night in Belgium, we were hit by a drunken driver trying to overtake a huge lorry on an impossible stretch of road. Our car would not be repaired quickly so, in order to reach Austria for scheduled meetings we had to find alternative transportation. As there were six of us, hitch-hiking was out of the question, but so was hiring a car in the remote area where we were stranded.

I telephoned a friend in Holland, and he said he could solve our problem by getting us a minibus. The question was how to get it to us. No problem, I assured him, we would pick it up ourselves. It was only after replacing the phone that I realised how impossible such a journey was going to be by public transport in the limited time available.

'You stay here,' I told the others, 'I'll hitch-hike to the nearest main-line station where I can pick up an international express train to Rotterdam. I'll be back with the minibus before you know it!'

One of the fellows wasn't happy about me going alone, so thoughtfully volunteered to go with me.

The hitch-hiking bit went well, and it was only when we were on the train that he suddenly realised his passport was back with the rest! We were fast approaching the Dutch frontier which has since relaxed its passport formalities, but then they were in full force. Officials were already aboard the train and working their way through the carriages examining passports. We were at a point of no return. Short of pulling the communication cord and making a dash for it, there was no way out.

Slowly and inexorably, the uniformed representatives of authority came through our long two-seats-a-side carriage until the one on our side was examining papers of the people closest to us. We were to be next!

Suddenly the official looked up from the passport he was holding. Something was wrong. He questioned the owner. Still unsatisfied, he walked back to check with a colleague. Their discussion continued until the train drew to a halt at the point where all the immigration officials got off. They never did ask for our passports.

Our delight lasted only until we finished telling our friend from whom we picked up the minibus. He shattered it with a simple question. 'How are you going to get back into Belgium?'

That's right! We still had a border to cross, minus one passport. And two people in a minibus were unlikely to be overlooked in quite the same way. What's more, it would be difficult to persuade the border officials that my friend's passport was already in their country. And we were so desperately short of time that there was no hope of one of our group bringing it to the border.

'Have fun!' said our Dutch friend, 'and don't forget you'll need to buy insurance to cover your transit across Belgium.'

That was it! The answer could be in the necessity to buy motor insurance at the border. Putting aside my friend's offer to hide in the back we drove on toward Belgium. Arriving at the frontier, I pulled alongside the inevitable official and beat him to his demand for passports by saying: 'Sir, we must buy insurance for this vehicle. Where can we do this?'

Momentarily swallowing his question, he pointed to the office. Then, before he could speak again, I asked brightly: 'Can we park there?'

'Yes,' he said, 'but . . . '

'I'm British,' I said, waving one of the passports he was trying to ask for, 'does that make any difference to my buying insurance?'

'No,' he replied, reaching for the passport.

Seemingly without thinking I pulled the passport out of his reach, opened the minibus door and jumped out beside him.

'But the vehicle is registered in Holland,' I insisted, pointing to the number plate but knowing it made no difference.

'That's perfectly all right, he said, still not having set hands on my passport.

'Oh thanks,' I exclaimed, disappearing into the office he had indicated.

My friend sat like a statue in the minibus, while the official suddenly realised that other car drivers were waiting for passport examination. He resumed his job with them.

Soon I reappeared with newly-purchased insurance papers in one hand and my passport in the other.

'Do you want to see these?' I called, waving the papers.

He stopped examining the passport he was holding, looked in my direction and shook his head wearily.

'What about this?' I asked, waving the passport.

'I've already seen that, haven't I?' he replied, beginning to sound a bit irked.

'Oh yes,' I agreed, 'so we're free to go now?'

'Yes,' he said turning back to the line of cars alongside him.

'Thanks!' I called, jumping into the minibus.

My friend only spoke when we were well clear of the border and safely inside Belgium.

'Phew!' he exclaimed with relief.

Just as I dislike hitch-hiking myself, I am reluctant to pick up hitch-hikers. If that sounds selfish, it isn't really. I'll give a ride to anyone I know, or anyone with whom I can establish reasonable contact first, but these days it can be asking for trouble to stop on a lonely Continental road and pick up a complete stranger. Nevertheless, I do make exceptions.

One day near home I saw a very well-dressed black man looking considerably agitated. On impulse I asked him if anything was wrong, even though he hadn't signalled me for help.

'Yes,' he said, 'my taxi hasn't arrived and I'm due to be at the airport in a few minutes.'

'Jump in,' I said, 'I'll get you there.'

'Thanks,' he said in relieved tones, 'but I have to make a detour to pick up something I'm taking with me.'

'Fine,' I said, 'you just tell me where and we'll go there first.'

On the way, he confided that he was personal assistant to the President of a certain African state. He had visited Geneva on official business and was now flying home. Soon we reached the place he was to pick up his still unidentified cargo. It was a dubious-looking private club. He dashed in and, moments later reappeared staggering beneath the load of a large crate of whisky!

'It's the President's favourite brand,' he explained breathlessly, as we resumed our trip to the airport. 'He'd never forgive me if I returned without it! But when I tell him how helpful you have been, I know he'll insist that you are a guest in the palace whenever you visit our country.'

I never have had cause to visit that particular country. And, as is the pattern in some of Africa's smaller States, the whisky-drinking President is no longer boss.

I'll concede the point that camping can be fun, but only when it is not a necessity. Some of our happiest camping experiences have been with friends in Spain. They provided all the equipment, including setting it up ready for our arrival and dismantling it at the end of the holiday. That's what I call carefree camping and, in a warm summer climate of which one can be sure, bad weather is no problem.

Probably soothed into a sense of security by such delightful experiences and urged by two children who insisted 'camping is fun', we invested in our own set of secondhand equipment. Borrowing a friend's lawn before we had our own, we practised erecting the tent and taking it down again. Thus rehearsed, we set out for a weekend of camping in Switzerland.

The area we chose offered no suitable camping site. So we drove on inspecting site after site. Either we were too choosey or the good sites were too crowded, but we wound up driving almost a complete circle before finishing the day in Montreux comparatively close to home. Tired and hungry, we erected our tent. Having done that we decided to forego cooking and cheat by going to a restaurant.

During our meal it began to rain. Before we finished it was literally bucketing down! The torrential rain was driving faster than we were as we made our way back to the camping site. Lightning flashed and thunder roared. I was feeling less like sleeping in that tent by the minute. Comforts of home were less than two hours away, but it was impossible to consider dismantling and repacking the tent in this deluge.

I cannot remember a more miserable night. I struggled into pyjamas only because my clothes were soaking wet. Then, before there was any chance to settle, I was splashing around outside the tent making frantic efforts to keep the thing standing. My sodden pyjamas clung uncomfortably to my soaked and miserable body.

When morning finally arrived, long hours later, we packed our things as fast as possible and headed for home. The equipment was never used again.

In younger and much madder days we once camped around central Europe while engaging in daily door-to-door literature distribution. One day we returned to our camping site to find gypsies there. Since we were not on a proper camping area, they had as much right to park their caravans as we had to pitch our tent. There was still room for us, and they were very friendly. We did, however, point out a police notice forbidding the parking of caravans there, and we added that the stringing of full clothes-lines between the trees was probably frowned on too. They thanked us for mentioning this, but said that they didn't mind if the police came and challenged them on the basis of the notice because they couldn't read anyway!

On one occasion a friend and I were stranded in Yugoslavia. Promised funds had not come through. Apart from a few cans of food in the back of the car we had hardly any assets. Our combined financial resources would probably just about buy enough petrol to get us home. But they left nothing for meals or accommodation.

The first night we slept in the car alongside a road in northern Italy. Our food was finished at breakfast-time. The second long, hungry day stretched before us. By evening, we were in the vicinity of some friends I knew would invite us for a meal. Phoning ahead, we explained we could only stop for a couple of hours, the truth being that we didn't wish to embarrass them by feeling they should share their own very limited accommodation with us.

The meal was greatly appreciated after the hot, foodless day and, as we finished and were preparing to leave, the question of where we would stay the night was raised.

'Oh, we'll press on,' we said, as convincingly as possible. We were dead tired.

'But, please stay,' said our friends, 'because when we heard you were coming we booked hotel rooms for you, and we want you to stay at our expense.'

They not only did a good thing for us but, without realising it, set a pattern I have followed many times since. The only difference is that the recipient has been some other needy friend for whom I have had the privilege of paying the bill.

Chapter Eight

COUNTING THE COST

Travel can be expensive, but the cost is not as high as most people think. For air travel it is the exception rather than the rule for me to pay full ordinary fare. And corners I cut on costs are available to anyone.

Stopovers en route can be made at no extra charge. Sometimes, depending on the mileage allowance of a particular ticket, detours can be made free or for little extra cost. To fly on certain evening flights between Monday and Thursday is cheaper than using the same flights Friday to Sunday. And both are considerably cheaper than flying morning or afternoon flights over the same routes in the same aircraft. Sometimes, to stay a minimum of six days in one place is cheaper than staying less. On transatlantic routes there are so many different ways of approaching fare structures that a good knowledgeable travel agent is essential. A European can fly U.S. domestic routes for only 50% of normal fares.

In my adopted home city of Geneva, my agent is a young lady with a second-to-none knowledge of the travel business. And within a stone's-throw of my Bristol office is the best travel agency in Britain! Even infrequent travellers do well to find a good agency which does its job at no cost to the customer (unless such things as special and expensive telephone calls are involved) because their income is derived from percentage pay-offs from companies whose tickets they sell.

One of the best-sounding travel bargains I ever found

was a 'See USA' ticket providing me with unlimited air travel for 21 days at a standard cost of $150. When checking in for a desired flight, a voucher was shown and a free ticket issued. It was possible to stay aloft for the entire 21 days if so desired, travelling from New York to Los Angeles, from Atlanta to Alaska and all points between, at no extra charge.

The catch? Only the so-called 'feeder' lines were participating in this arrangement. These are smaller companies, of which there are many in the U.S., covering local areas and bringing passengers to larger airports serviced by the big transcontinental lines. By these little lines it is possible to cover the entire country, but whereas the larger lines fly big long-haul jets, the 'feeders' run 'hedge-hoppers' which put down at every landing strip in sight.

Experience taught me that such a ticket is all right if the total itinerary is in comparatively short, consecutive hops, but being stuck with it for a coast-to-coast flight isn't funny!

I once flew from Buffalo to Seattle in this way. It took me two days, six airlines and 24 landings and take-offs. I arrived at my destination having lost the voucher which would enable me to continue trips of this kind for the next 19 days. By that time I was past caring! (Someone found the voucher behind a plane seat and was unfeeling enough to return it to me a few days later!)

On a mile-for-mile comparison I find that air travel is usually cheaper than using a car, and the time-saving makes it even more attractive. Of course, I need a good, serviceable car for the many journeys on which I am carrying more than I can by plane. And if two or more people are travelling by car it can be cheaper. But if I drive myself between London and Geneva, carrying no more baggage than is my normal allowance by plane, it is considerably cheaper to fly.

In Christian service economy is a key factor in travel planning. Tight budgets have always precluded the possibility of flying First Class, and I have no desperate desire to do so anyway. But, on a few memorable occasions I have been elevated to the ranks of the elite without having to pay the price!

When stranded by a regular commercial airline, the company at fault is committed to providing alternative passage to the required destination. I reminded a counter clerk of this when I was stranded by a broken-down plane at a midwestern city of the United States. In such circumstances delays are usually minimal. Invariably there is another company flying to the same destination, or a possible rerouting to achieve the same objective.

I was going to the West Coast and discovered that another airline flying much better planes had a flight to my destination in the next half-hour. The counter clerk of the line which had let me down picked up his telephone to call the other desk and see if I could be transferred.

After making the request, he listened a moment, then put his hand over the mouthpiece and said to me: 'They say they have only one First Class seat.'

'I'll take it,' I said, clutching my Economy Class ticket.

'He'll take it,' he said into the telephone. Then, as he replaced the receiver he tooked startled and said: 'Hey, wait a minute! We're paying for this!'

'That's right,' I agreed with a benign smile.

With a look of defeated resignation, he sighed: 'O.K. you win.'

On another occasion, the airline I was travelling overbooked Economy Class so I was fortunate enough to be asked to move to First Class for one short leg of a much longer journey. At the intermediate stopping point, I was told, many Economy Class passengers would be getting off and I could return to my more accustomed area of the plane. The problem was that by the time we reached that point, I was very comfortably settled in my more spacious First Class seat.

When the stewardess came to escort me back to Economy Class I had the audacity to ask her: 'What would you say if I told you I'd rather stay here for the rest of the flight?'

For a brief moment she looked surprised, and then she smiled.

'I'd say . . . how about another cup of coffee!'

I accepted gratefully and stayed put.

First Class only tempts me when it is almost empty and Economy Class is jammed full. Then it looks like a welcome oasis of tranquility in a sea of seething turmoil. This was especially so when I boarded a pre-Christmas flight from London to Geneva. I was late, and the last passenger to board at the front entrance. I walked through the cool serenity of a deserted First Class compartment to be faced by the crushed humanity in Economy Class. The sardine image was helped by Christmas packages which seemed to be on laps, between feet, in fact filling almost every spare space.

Unenthusiastically I searched for the one empty seat I knew must be there, but without success. Every seat was taken, even though I was carrying a confirmed Economy Class ticket. I shared my problem with a kindly stewardess who promptly solved it by saying: 'You'd better move into First Class then.'

Strangely enough, I have not found this to be such an isolated incident. More than once since then, when I have been booked on an obviously full flight and passengers are shoving like bull elephants to board first and get their favourite seats, I have sat back in the departure lounge until last. Then, with the nonchalant air of one who knows where he's going, I board with my Economy Class boarding card to be met by an apologetic stewardess who says: 'It seems as if all Economy Class seats are taken.' After briefly commiserating with her, I accept her suggestion of going through to First!

But the fact remains that although on occasions I have a First Class heart I've learned to live with an Economy Class budget. Sometimes, especially in my early days of travelling, even an economy fare has been more than I could afford. At such times, when a journey must be made, the matter of the deficit is turned over to a Heavenly Accountant. On several occasions I remember being able to scrape together only enough for a one-way ticket, travelling to some distant place and telling the Lord: 'I believe you want me there, so I'm trusting you to get me back!'

Since the advent of credit cards, the likelihood of being stranded is removed. Concern about how to cover the return fare is delayed at least a month. This makes it possible to wonder where the deficit is coming from in the comfort of home!

While credit cards are a boon to the international traveller spending in many different currencies, they do take the cliff-hanging aspect out of waiting for God's provision.

Once, in pre-credit card days, I was sharing a hotel room with Leslie Edgell, who is now British Director of the Slavic Gospel Association. We came to the end of our stay calculating that we were well short of the cash needed to cover our bill. Income on the evangelistic tour we shared had fallen far short of our initial predictions. With check-out time less than two hours away, there was only one thing left to do.

'Lord,' I prayed fervently as we knelt together in the room, 'you know our predicament and only you can solve it.'

I went on to inform the Lord that since the Bible confirms 'the cattle upon a thousand hills' are his, surely it was a small thing for him to cover our hotel bill. At this point Leslie confessed to an 'unsanctified' vision of us picking up the bill at the desk and informing the cashier that payment was tethered to the fence outside!

We went down to breakfast. Walking into the dining room, we met an evangelist who, until now, we had known only by reputation. Likewise, he had seen our pictures in some Christian periodical and identified us. We were soon eating together and enjoying the kind of Christian fellowship which made us forget momentarily the harsh realities of a fast-approaching hour of reckoning.

Finishing breakfast, our new friend said: 'It's been great to meet you both. How about us all going to my room for some prayer before we separate?'

Good idea, we agreed, and followed him upstairs.

Back on our knees we were reminded of our previous prayer session which, until now, had seemingly been fruitless. But neither of us dreamed of referring to this in the presence of this man. We prayed about things in general, about each other's work and many other things. Then, suddenly, our friend interrupted by leaping to his feet and, without warning, announcing: 'The Lord told me to pay your bill!'

Startled, I looked at Leslie and he looked at me. This couldn't be the answer to our prayers. This man was a fellow-evangelist and probably almost as close to being destitute as we were!

'But . . . ' we both began to protest at once.

'No refusals,' he interrupted, 'if God tells me to do it, you mustn't stop me!'

Who were we to argue?

God's provision sometimes involves split-second timing and divinely-ordained 'coincidence' . . . like the day my self-drive hire-car broke down in the middle of London. I was travelling north with a considerable amount of equipment and a tight time schedule. The car couldn't be repaired immediately. The company was unable to provide another. There was nothing for it but to get a taxi to the railway station from which an express train was leaving within the next hour. According to my calculations, I could just make it to my evening meeting if I managed to catch this.

Once aboard the taxi, I relaxed as we sped through London's traffic . . . but only briefly. Suddenly I realised that I had no money for the train fare! In fact, it was questionable if I could muster sufficient even to pay off the taxi. The car had a full tank which would have got me to my destination but I had little extra money with me.

'I'll need to stop at a bank,' I told the taxi driver.

I had no idea how this would help because I had no bank account. So, when the driver asked me which bank, I told him any would do! I didn't know how I was going to solve my problem once inside a bank, but at least this was a place where there was money and that was what I was in desperate need of at that moment.

There was no time to work out careful strategy before the driver came to stop outside a bank he chose at random. What's more, time was at a premium because the train for which I couldn't afford a ticket, but was imperative to catch, was leaving shortly. I rushed through the doors to the nearest counter, sending up a telegraphic 'Lord help me' prayer as I went.

I had no time to wonder how to approach the counter clerk on the delicate subject of why he should provide me, a perfect stranger, with money for a train ticket. The reason being that the fellow behind the counter looked up and said: 'You're Dave Foster aren't you?'

I couldn't believe it! I'd never seen him in my life before. But I quickly admitted my identity, at the same time noting he was wearing a Scripture Union badge.

'I thought it was you,' he said, pleased with himself, 'because I've often seen your picture in various Christian papers. What can I do for you?'

Embarrassment dissolved as I realised here was a sympathetic fellow Christian. Before I finished explaining my predicament, he was reaching into his pocket to loan me the needed money.

These days my constant international travel, especially to countries requiring separate visas for every entry, means that my passport fills very quickly. A British passport is valid for ten years . . . theoretically. But fill it in less than two years, as I do invariably, and a new one must be obtained. A new passport costs five pounds whether it lasts for ten years or two, so whereas it costs the average Britisher fifty pence a year to have one, mine works out at five times as much!

'I'm beginning to resent this,' I told a Passport Office cashier on one of my bi-annual visits. 'At this rate, I fork out twenty-five pounds in ten years where other people get by for five!'

She was unimpressed and unsympathetic.

'Anyone who can afford to travel enough to fill passports as fast as you do, can afford a fiver for a new one!'

If only she knew.

Chapter Nine

GO NOW – PAY LATER!

Credit cards have been defined as 'small pieces of plastic designed to encourage people to spend more'. They have their disadvantages when placed in irresponsible and undisciplined hands, but benefits outweigh their burdens for the average travelling man.

I have a love/hate relationship with the system they represent. It is a boon in minimising the amount of money I carry, and credit cards are not as bulky, costly and complicated as travellers' cheques. They are a constant help in overcoming currency changes when dodging from one country to another. Expenses charged to a credit card anywhere ultimately find their way on to a single monthly bill reduced to the common denominator of home currency.

The cards have many other advantages, some of which hadn't occurred to me. Pulling into a Los Angeles filling station I saw a large sign: 'AFTER 7 PM, CORRECT CHANGE & CREDIT CARDS ONLY. HELP STOP ROBBERIES.'

These cards are a curse to those who cannot control their spending. Someone suggested that the 'buy now – pay later' attraction they project would be dimmed if they were called by the more accurate name of 'debit cards'.

Advertisements for them seem to pander to materialistic instincts. One card offers to take 'the waiting out of wanting', and coloured advertisements show people enjoying expensive luxury items without a trace of worry about how they'll meet the day of reckoning.

Even the delayed shock of being confronted with a fat bill is minimised with the invitation to 'let it ride'. The full amount does not have to be paid immediately, the customer is told. Delay in payment only results in a fiddling little 1½% being charged for the privilege next month. But if the fellow with expensive new hi-fi he can't afford will lower its volume to a level conducive to clear thinking, he'll wake up to the fact that such charges mount up to a whacking 18% in the course of a single year!

Some suggest that in time credit cards may make actual money obsolete. That may be wishful thinking by the companies operating them. Certainly one man tried to prove the point by going about his normal course of living for a month without using money. With the help of more than fifty credit cards, he succeeded. It's hardly necessary to add that such a feat could only be accomplished in the United States . . . at the moment.

Experiments are being made in Europe where it will be possible to put a credit card in a slot on the side of a filling station pump and serve yourself with petrol. The amount is automatically charged, but the customer does not receive a bill. Instead, a central computer records the purchase, communicates it to another computer at the bank of the customer where the appropriate sum is automatically transferred from his account to that of the filling station. Even that may be 'improved' by a further automatic process in which the amount is transferred direct to the petrol company, the retailer's share being deducted along the way!

Such heavy reliance on computers creates nightmare thoughts of complications caused by error. Credit card companies already rely on computers for billing, and a single error can be multiplied alarmingly. One business executive advised me: 'If your account ever gets messed up, the only way out is to close it, sort out the problem and then start all over again.'

So far I have encountered only one small error in this way, and that was difficult enough to get rectified. Finally, in desperation, I wrote pleading for a human being to deal with the matter! Then, tongue in cheek, I added: 'My regards to your computer'. The human being who did sort it out satisfactorily showed a sense of humour too by assuring me that 'our computer reciprocates your greetings and thanks you for your understanding'!

I thought that credit cards were peculiar to capitalist societies until I found them being accepted in Eastern Europe. Not that the average East European would be issued with one, but accepting this form of payment from Western businessmen and tourists increases the influx of hard currency which Communist governments desperately need.

New travellers east should be warned that things are not always what they seem to be in these areas. When short of cash in one rural East European town, I knew it would be helpful in conserving my dwindling resources by finding a hotel which accepted credit cards. Whereas in Western Europe such a solution would be easy, even in the smaller towns these days, the acceptance of credit cards in Eastern Europe is usually limited to the larger cities and main tourist areas. So I was surprised to find what I was looking for . . . a modest hotel displaying a window sticker of the major credit card company of which I am a member. I checked in.

Came the dawn, and my departure. Confidently I handed the hotel cashier my credit card to settle the account. She looked baffled and asked what it was for. Now I was baffled!

'Your hotel is displaying a large sign indicating you accept payment by means of this credit card,' I explained. 'Are you seriously suggesting you don't recognise it?'

'I've never seen one before,' she said.

The receptionist was called for her advice. She was equally ignorant of the whole system which I proceeded to explain in detail and which they both agreed was 'a good idea'.

'But why is your hotel advertising its affiliation to this company when it doesn't know the first thing about credit cards?' I asked.

'Oh that!' exclaimed the receptionist when I pointed to the sign in the window. 'Our manager made a trip to the West and brought it back as a souvenir. He said that most of the hotels he saw there were displaying them!'

Perhaps my own credit card philosophy is best demonstrated by the fact that I never use them at home. They are functional for travelling, but in the place where I live we have a self-imposed rule that 'if we can't pay cash, we can't have it'.

It puts waiting into wanting. But sometimes that period proves that the 'want' is not a 'need'. And if we finally reach a point of acquisition we appreciate it so much more!

Chapter Ten

DEFECTOR OR SKYJACKER?

The small East European plane in which I was flying prepared to land. The seat belt sign suddenly lit up and the stewardess made a landing announcement.

'We'll be about ten minutes early in Vienna,' I thought as I glanced at my watch. 'Must have had the wind behind us!'

I was sitting on an aisle seat so did not look out of the window. Otherwise I would have realised that the airport below was not Vienna. The moment we touched down, I knew it . . . even before the captain spoke to us.

'Ladies and gentlemen, this is your captain speaking . . .'

The disembodied voice from the speaker above me sounded strangely urgent.

'Please listen carefully. This is *not* Vienna. While airborne we received orders to . . . '

Skyjack! The obvious conclusion sprang to mind, but one thing didn't add up. We had just returned to our starting point. No skyjacker would order that.

'It is imperative that all passengers remain in their seats,' continued the captain. 'Security forces are about to board the aircraft.'

The plane had stopped taxiing at a remote part of the airfield. As I glanced out of the window, I froze. We were surrounded by uniformed gunmen!

Sitting in the very back row of seats, I was right at the hub of the action when our stewardess opened the door and a plainclothesman jumped in. He was covered by two armed guards.

'Passports!' he yelled down the plane in what I thought was rather an odd request.

I fumbled for mine and he took it. Just as he was examining it, a young man toward the front of the plane disobeyed the captain's order and stood up. He called something I couldn't understand, and the official stopped looking at my passport. Without taking his eyes off the young man, he dropped it in my lap.

I slid down until I was barely able to see over the seat back in front as the young man stepped into the aisle and stood facing the official alongside me. No one moved. The plane was in complete silence. The atmosphere tense. Armed guards behind the official looked uncertain. Then the young man began walking along the aisle with his hands held away from his body. For an illogical moment I thought the official was embracing him, but then realised he was actually frisking him. No weapon was found.

As the young man left the plane and was taken away in a waiting police vehicle, a hubbub of multilingual conversation broke out among the passengers. The stewardess explained the whole incident to me in English.

The young man had tried to defect. It wasn't premeditated. Arriving at the airport that morning, he checked in to fly to another East European destination. Then, quite unexpectedly, he saw a flight ticket another passenger had dropped. Quickly he scooped it up and saw it was for Vienna. He could never have bought a ticket to a West European destination, but here he was holding one. A plan quickly formulated in his mind.

He used it to check in at another counter to Vienna. No problem. He now held a boarding pass for the Vienna flight, but he still faced a problem. At Passport Control he would have to show the boarding pass together with his East European passport. This would be fatal to his plan. The solution was to show his *other* boarding pass for the legitimate flight to his original East European destination.

Once past passport officials he stood in the departure lounge waiting not for his own flight to be called, but for the Vienna departure. The East European boarding pass which had brought him this far was now stuffed in his pocket and the Vienna boarding pass brought out. A last hurdle stood between him and freedom, personified by the last official checking boarding passes before passsengers actually went to their appropriate planes. His Vienna pass lacked one thing . . . the official stamp of the passport controller.

Amazingly, the man who checked it did not query the fact and, as I boarded my plane that morning, I had no idea that just ahead of me was a fellow passenger whose heart must have been thumping so hard he was afraid everyone else would hear it! For him it must have been an eternity before the plane was closed, taxied and took off.

I wondered if he had guessed anything when we landed again, or whether he could scarcely contain his excitement thinking we were in Vienna.

What happened on the ground during all this? How was the discovery made? When were we ordered to return?

The person who lost the Vienna ticket discovered it when he tried to check in. He reported the loss but resigned himself to the fact that he would not be on that particular flight. There was a later flight to Vienna so, after sorting out the ticket problem, he would transfer to that. Meanwhile various officials checked if the ticket had turned up in the Lost Property Office or was passed in at any other counter. Suddenly it occurred to someone that the now airborne Vienna flight had left full whereas, with one passenger still sitting in the airport, it should have had one empty seat!

The plane was still under orders from the departure

airport's tower. A quick call was put through to confirm the flight was full. An affirmative answer came back from our puzzled crew who had expected a full flight anyway. The pilot was baffled by the next order – to return immediately, and then he was warned that one of his passengers must be a stowaway! Not knowing that the intruder was a quiet, unarmed would-be defector, the pilot realised that he could be carrying an armed skyjacker or some other dangerous person. No wonder he made a very wide and gentle turn to land at our take-off point without a word to passengers before they and whoever was the intruder could see we were surrounded by armed guards!

The incident reminded me of the many people who ask me, 'Aren't you scared to fly these days?' The question usually comes from grounded-and-glad-of-it friends who daily risk their necks in the statistically more dangerous business of car travel.

I remember one stewardess giving the following landing announcement: 'Ladies and gentlemen, we have just landed at – . If you are continuing by road, may we remind you that the safest part of your journey has just been completed. So drive carefully!'

I was reminded that driving a taxi in some places can be more dangerous than flying a plane these days. A sign inside Philadelphia's yellow cabs says: 'Driver has no more than $5 in change. Cab equipped with safe – Driver cannot open it.'

Naturally the air traveller is aware of risks greater than that of mechanical failure these days. But if God's promises are true and divine protection is a practical thing, I'd be a strange kind of Christian if I were afraid to board a plane. That doesn't mean I discount the possibility of one day being reported the victim of a wild-eyed anarchist, but if it ever happens I'll know it was preceded by a divine nod of approval and is all a part of his eternal plan.

That doesn't mean I am ungrateful for the many security measures now in operation, but none can be completely effective. Some are quite amusing!

For instance, bombs in airports can be an equal threat to bombs in planes. In one building I know, bureaucracy went mad with the issuing of a three-page set of instructions on what to do if someone telephones a bomb threat. The employee receiving the call is asked to complete a form with the following information:

1. Time the call was received and concluded.
2. Exact words used to make the threat.
3. When the bomb is set to explode.
4. Where the bomb is located. Actual physical location within the building.
5. What kind of bomb? What does it look like? How large is it? What kind of triggering device; pressure; chemical delay; time clock; electrical? Is it composed of liquid chemicals such as nitroglycerine or solids such as black powder?
6. Reason for placing the bomb.
7. Descriptive information relating to the caller and location of call: male or female, approximate age, speech impediments, accents, language used, background noises, additional remarks.

The mind boggles! My vivid imagination sees some minor employee, phone clamped to ear, writing furiously and asking: 'Would you mind repeating details of the triggering device? Just as you were saying it the first time I was deafened by an explosive noise from another part of the building!'

Or: 'You say it's under a desk in the accounts department. How coincidental! That's where I'm sitting right now!'

And a possible follow-through on the last one: 'If you can just hang on a minute, perhaps I should dash to the other end of the building and complete this call on another line!'

Instructions on what to do in an airborne crisis are more difficult to formulate, and various airlines have different ideas on how to deal with skyjackers. These range from those who say 'do everything he orders' to the intransigent Israelis who maintain a firm policy of non-cooperation with anarchists. If that sounds scaring, I should add that when I have the choice of flying EL AL, I take it every time. It's the safest and most security conscious airline in the world!

One small and rather innovative airline dealt with its first skyjacker in a unique way. He was overpowered by a crew member who then, either on higher orders or his own initiative, took the prisoner into the empty First Class cabin, strapped him into a seat, wrapped a towel around his neck and slit his throat!

Security begins on the ground and today's air traveller may be subjected to all kinds of checks. Apart from straightforward frisking and examination of hand-baggage, some airports have electronic devices to indicate if a passenger is carrying metal when he walks through. One of these which the Swiss were using but seem to have abandoned has a warning light that comes on when metal is detected. The first time I went through this contraption, it lit up. Puzzled at first, I then fished out my bunch of keys, handed it to the security man and went through again. It still lit up.

'Any other metal on you?' he asked.

I was already pulling off my wedding ring, a plastic ballpoint pen with a metal clasp and other minor pieces of metal which should not have been enough to activate it. Finally, free of it all, I stepped through again with a confidence which was immediately shattered by that exasperating little light.

'Tooth fillings?' I asked the security man.

'*Non*, *impossible*!' he replied, scratching his head.

'Too much iron in my blood!' I suggested helpfully.

'*Pas du tout*', he muttered, having taken me seriously.

Still baffled, but not doubting my basic integrity, he waved me on. Neither was the machine at fault because on subsequent occasions I always succeeded in lighting up similar devices. I still don't know why.

'If you were of the female sex,' said another puzzled security man, 'I could understand it.'

He went on to explain, in rather hushed and embarrassed tones for a Continental I thought, that certain garments peculiar to what he insisted calling 'the female sex' contained innocent but functional pieces of metal.

The Swiss certainly take security seriously. At one time signs in several languages were posted on departure lounge doors at Geneva Airport beginning: 'You are now entering a military area . . . ' They went on to explain that armed soldiers were on duty and, if they gave an order to halt, immediate obedience was necessary. The warning continued that they had instructions to open fire at the first refusal to obey such a command. I often wondered how many elderly passengers, on seeing that, turned up the volume control on their hearing aids before venturing on to the tarmac!

Soon after the dreadful massacre in Tel Aviv airport, air travellers seemed to get a little edgy in any arrival area where Japanese passengers were waiting for baggage. Again the Swiss attempted to put minds at rest. When I went to meet my wife from a London flight, I noticed she and her fellow passengers at the incoming baggage belt were subjected to the close scrutiny of a nearby guard holding a submachine gun at the ready.

Veteran air passengers are now used to hearing final flight calls with the added warning that security checks will be in operation. Such announcements are usually worded carefully so as to maintain an air of normality and not cause undue concern to any timid types, but only a British mind could come up with the announcement I heard at Heathrow. After warning that we would again be asked to produce passports, boarding cards and flight tickets, the announcer went on to say that handbaggage 'will be searched for any foreign objects not conducive to air travel'!

The procedure of going through a small cubicle for searching in an airport lounge is one I have been through scores of times. Kloten Airport at Zurich, one I pass through frequently, has a whole line of cubicles neatly divided for men and women. The formula is simple. Step inside with the security man (or lady, according to the passenger's sex), have handbaggage opened and examined, then hold up arms for a complete frisking of body and legs.

So when I saw two newly-erected cubicles in Budapest Airport, it was no surprise. Male and female passengers formed two long lines which seemed to be going through at remarkable speed. My turn came. I stepped in with the uniformed policeman. As he pulled the curtain to ensure privacy, I was beginning to open my briefcase.

'No, no,' he said when he saw what I was doing, and indicated that he didn't want to see what I was carrying.

I shrugged and lifted my arms for the customary personal check.

He smiled and shook his head.

'Have a good flight,' he said, and waved me on without a question.

Trusting people, those Hungarians!

Chapter Eleven

'WE REGRET TO ANNOUNCE . . .'

The possibility of skyjacking is usually more remote from the mind of the frequent air traveller than more mundane problems connected with this mode of transportation.

Delays are the most common. Often these are due to weather conditions, but sometimes it is because of such things as a strike by air traffic controllers in a country which may not be your destination but over whose air-space your flight must travel. Mechanical problems can also crop up from time to time, although I am always rather thankful when these are discovered on the ground *before* we are airborne.

Most airlines provide passengers with free refreshments during a delay. Sometimes a full meal is served at appropriate times of day. Rare overnight delays sometimes involve the airline in the costly business of providing hotel accommodation.

The keenness of airline competition causes some to develop frustrating habits when delays are inevitable. For instance, if an airline knows there will be a delay or diversion when the passenger is checking in they rarely admit it. Once a person is checked in with his heavy baggage in custody of the airline, it is assumed that he is less likely to switch to a rival line when he discovers the delay. What's more, some airlines deliberately avoid announcing changes of plan until time for the final call for passengers. At this stage, having passed through passport control and loaded himself with duty-free shopping, the poor passenger feels he's reached the point of no return and is at the mercy of the airline.

I can forgive most airline idiosyncracies along this line except downright lying. Waiting for one flight from a certain airport to Geneva, an announcement was made of delayed departure due to fog at our destination. It's logical to delay take-off rather than later having to circle the destination airport until fog clears. This is acceptable and, on this occasion, it was indicated that the delay was unlikely to be long. Presumably the Geneva fog was clearing.

I went to a phone to call my wife and warn her not to come to the airport without checking our new arrival time.

'We're delayed because of the fog at Geneva airport,' I explained.

'Fog?' she replied from our home, less than ten minutes from the airport, 'there's no fog here. It's a beautifully clear evening!'

As I left the phone box, another passenger came out of the next one. He looked baffled.

'Just talked to my wife in Lausanne,' he said. 'She had just telephoned Geneva Airport to check my arrival time and was told all air traffic is running on schedule.'

Dark doubts about the integrity of the airline on which we were booked crossed our minds. There was a delay, but it wasn't for the reason announced. So the problem must be mechanical or something else. But why the lying? Suddenly a likely theory occurred to me. A SWISSAIR flight was scheduled for a little later. The airline on which we were travelling was afraid its own delay would result in many passengers switching to SWISSAIR, but if they announced 'fog in Geneva' passengers would assume that the Swiss airline would suffer similar delay so why bother to change?

Whether or not that was a correct assessment, I cannot be sure. But it still seems the only logical reason for lying.

I went back to the desk where passengers were milling around and having their questions answered by airline officials. I made my way through the crowd to the desk and, as pleasantly as possible, asked to be transferred to SWISSAIR.

All conversation stopped. Other passengers stared. The girls behind the desk looked at me as if I'd uttered a bad word.

'But sir,' said one in the kind of despairing tone she may have reserved for someone educationally subnormal, 'what good will that do you?'

'It will get me to Geneva,' I replied.

'But sir,' she began again, 'if our flight is delayed due to fog in Geneva, SWISSAIR will be subject to similar delay.'

She'd asked for it, even though I was reluctant to embarrass her.

'There is no fog in Geneva,' I said with quiet authority.

She glanced uneasily at the other passengers who were now listening with interest.

'But sir,' she began for the third time, 'didn't you hear the announcement?'

'Yes,' I said, 'and since then I heard my wife on the telephone from Geneva tell me the weather is perfectly clear there.'

I felt sorry for the girl. She was the victim of higher authority. I'm even prepared to believe that she didn't know the truth. She believed the official line as we were expected to. But I still switched to SWISSAIR, and at least twenty other passengers followed my lead.

I am sure that my unwitting boosting of SWISSAIR's revenue that day has no bearing on the attractive plaque which now graces my office wall, signed by the President of SWISSAIR, 'to certify that' I have 'been appointed a member of the Swissair Travel Club in appreciation of the friendly attitude shown toward our company and frequent use of our line'.

Let's face it. With international control and competition there are no *really* bad airlines. There are a few I avoid whenever possible, but none I would refuse to fly under any circumstances.

Some are plagued by problems beyond their control. In these days of industrial unrest and union militancy, I would even put some strikes in that classification. At one period, AIR FRANCE was dogged by so many work stoppages that regular passengers suggested it be renamed AIR CHANCE. BEA has had its share of disputes as well and, sympathetic as I am, I couldn't help being amused by an Osbert Lancaster cartoon after one of these. It showed a couple of passengers listening to an airport announcement: 'British European Airways regret to announce that the emergency is now over and that all further delays will be due to the usual causes.'

Once aboard the aircraft, there are other problems which face some travellers. I remember a first-time air traveller with tendencies toward claustrophopia who asked the stewardess: 'Isn't it possible to open a window in here?'

Although I have only heard of it actually happening once, some are scared of getting on the wrong plane! The safeguards against this are such as to make it almost completely impossible, but the fact that 'anything can happen' seemed to be endorsed by an inveterate practical joker of my acquaintance.

Airlines used to have a practice, now seemingly discontinued, of having the captain complete a pro forma flight log, a single piece of paper which was then passed from passenger to passenger back through the plane. It gave such information as weather conditions en route, altitude of flight, estimated time of arrival and the destination. The fellow I knew would get this sheet passed to him during a flight . . . and pocket it. Passengers behind would be none the wiser because it was never generally announced that the information sheet was being circulated, neither was it expected to be returned to the captain. Presumably the last passenger could keep it as a souvenir.

Having intercepted and kept it, the practical joker would preserve it carefully until his next flight when, at a respectable time after take-off he would pass it to passengers behind him. The effect on people fondly believing they were going to Lisbon suddenly to see something like 'Destination: Helsinki' had to be seen to be believed! Or so he told me.

My pet gripe about air travel is sometimes being forced to sit beside a smoker whose wretched pipe or cigarette always seems to waft smoke across my meal and in my face. I give full marks to airlines such as LUFTHANSA and FINNAIR which now reserve three or four rows at the front of the cabin for non-smokers.

Some air travellers are fanatics about their seat preferences. Whereas one man dives for a window seat, others much prefer to sit by the aisle. Surprisingly few seem to catch on to the fact that there is more leg room in seats alongside emergency exits. I'll never forget the little old lady who was ushered on to a BEA Trident ahead of me. Obviously her first flight, she was already enjoying every minute of it . . . even before she was airborne.

'Where would you like to sit madam?' asked a helpful stewardess.

'Don't mind at all, m'dear,' chirped the old soul, 'as long as I'm facing the engine!'

Safety features and emergency procedures are spelled out to each passenger on cards in the seat pockets, but it's surprising how few bother to read them. Perhaps this is a mute endorsement of faith in the safety of air travel. An interesting difference I've noticed between many U.S. and European airlines is the way in which they present these things. Obviously it is unwise to panic a timid passenger by heading the card 'What To Do When Crashing', but

European airlines usually take a more positive line like 'Safety In The Air'. Their American counterparts, on the other hand, tend to go to the other extreme with such titles as 'Comforting Facts'.

Air sickness is almost a thing of the past with smooth-flying jets which often avoid bad weather by flying above it. But airlines still play safe in providing plastic lined bags for their more unfortunate customers. TWA quietly demonstrates how rarely they are used for their primary purpose by actually printing on them Gin Rummy Scorecards!

The effects of long-distance jet flight and resulting time changes are not so easily overcome. The body cannot be adjusted as quickly as a watch. Sleep cycles are upset, and various biological functions need to change gear. Some companies advise their top executives not to make important decisions too soon after arriving in a new time zone.

These problems will be compounded by supersonic travel. It will be strange, to say the least, to complete a three-hour flight from London to New York, arriving at a local time of two hours *before* your watch claims you departed. Could the supersonic traveller going west around the world arrive at his original point of departure before leaving? Pretty soon we'll be getting buried before we're born!

Another long-flight hazard is stiffness and backache. FINNAIR has faced the matter squarely and explains to passengers in a printed leaflet that 'circulation and metabolism may deteriorate during long periods of sitting . . . slowing down of the circulation of venous blood can cause numbness of the limbs.'

'For this reason,' we are told (and because 'Finnair has always held passenger comfort to be an important matter'), 'the Institute of Occupational Health has planned a short series of exercises which are likely to be very beneficial during long flights.'

For sake of interest, it may be as well to describe these simple exercises which, for the life of me, I've never actually brought myself to engage in.

The first is: 'Raise the heels and stretch the ankles vigorously. Rotate the ankles. Curl and stretch the toes.' All simple stuff which can be accomplished discreetly without attracting the attention of passengers alongside.

But I wonder what the person in the next seat would think to see me suddenly 'stretch the back, turning the right shoulder towards the right and breathing in at the same time.' By the time I get to 'Relax and exhale' it could have given him a nasty turn! Then when I 'repeat the exercise to the left', he'd probably be surreptitiously reaching for the call button to summon a stewardess. And before I could 'pull stomach in whilst flexing the sedentary muscles' she'd probably have me in a straitjacket!

Most of my flights are within Europe, so I don't have to face the trauma of major time changes or the effects of sitting in one place for an inordinately long period of time. Probably my major concern is summed up in a description of the benefits of air travel which goes 'breakfast in Beirut, lunch in London, dinner in Dallas . . . and baggage in Bombay!'

With increasing numbers of air travellers, frequency of services and size of planes, the problems of ensuring that a passenger's baggage is actually loaded aboard the flight on which he travels become more difficult. Although any delay or misdirection is usually only temporary, it can be most inconvenient.

I can appreciate the sentiment of the man who, seeing his friend off at the airport, said: 'May God and your baggage go with you!'

Chapter Twelve

FASTEN YOUR SEATBELT, COMRADE!

Someone said: 'The main characteristics of air travel are dullness and danger.'

Journalist James Cameron seems to concur when he writes in his autobiography (POINT OF DEPARTURE – Panther Books): 'I began to feel that my life was spent tethered to an inclinable seat, peering without pleasure at the planet below, listening with amateur anxiety to the whine and mutter of engines I neither understood nor trusted. After millions of miles I understand them no better; the theory of aerodynamics is reasonable, but there is still no explanation of how the wings stay on.'

Cameron is far ahead of me in notching up air miles, but I must admit that I have long since ceased to be aware of engine noises, unless there is any variation in their usual steady sound. I do confess to a tinge of 'amateur anxiety' when, climbing aboard my first Russian-built Tupolev-134, I picked up a glossy brochure informing me 'high-powered engines provide for safe take-off even under unfavourable meteorological conditions. Moreover, the flight can be smoothly and safely continued even in the case of one engine failure.' Strange how a line designed to reassure sometimes has the opposite effect!

When INTERFLUG, the East German airline, began using this aircraft they had a journalist aboard the first flight to report his impressions. His piece, in English, for their publicity magazine, included the following: ' "It is great fun to work under such conditions", was the concise answer to my question about the flight characteristics of the TU-134. What surprises did the flight hold in store for the passengers, I wanted to know of the chief pilot. "The passengers may have differing expectations, but there will be something for everybody".

Having travelled just about every East European airline, I know what he means! Listing a number of cities, Russia's AEROFLOT timetable informed me 'between these points the airline does not enjoy commercial flights'. I could have added a number of other cities between which I didn't enjoy flights! The most memorable was when jet exhaust fumes began seeping in through the ventilation ducts. I gazed bemused at this unusual sight, and amazed that the stewardesses appeared not to notice and simply kept on serving meals. Soon the passengers were coughing as the cabin filled with this obnoxious haze. By this time the stewardesses had disappeared, and I began to wonder if they had baled out! I pushed the call button but it didn't work. Fumes were now seeping through cracks in the cabin upholstery as well. Suddenly I saw a stewardess appear through the swirling, eye-stinging mist. She appeared to be blissfully ignoring all that was happening. I grabbed her arm and, unable to speak, pointed at the dense fumes still belching through my ventilator. In the encircling gloom I caught a quick flash of silver tooth as she gave me what was supposed to be a reassuring smile. Then she disappeared again.

Minutes later we landed and, eyes streaming, throat choking, staggered out into the fresh air of Frankfurt Airport. I never did get an explanation of the incident. The airline concerned preferred to pretend it never happened!

TIME Magazine once devoted an entire article to East European airlines. It began with this story: 'It was a clear day over Eastern Europe, and the piston-engined Ilyushin 14 plane of TAROM, the Rumanian airline, was flying smoothly on course from Bucharest to Constantia, Rumania. All at once, the plane began pitching and banking erratically. While passengers paled, the captain stepped out of the forward cabin and plopped into a vacant seat. "The comrade director," he explained, "is a very nice man and likes to try his hand at flying." '

So far as I am aware, no 'comrade director' has ever flown a plane in which I was a passenger, but I can believe TIME's claim that 'quite a few Eastern European pilots flew fighters for either the British or Russians during World War II, and have never lost their Spitfire habits'. I must admit though, that their safety records are regarded as average. And this in itself is a miracle when one sees some of the planes they are expected to fly. Many people have found the following story hard to believe, but I can vouch for the absolute accuracy of every detail. Only actual names and places have been omitted to protect the guilty!

A full contingent of passengers walked across the tarmac of one of Western Europe's smaller airports to board an ancient prop plane which I failed to identify. It was a thick, stubby-looking thing with a rear passenger entrance alongside a very high tail. We were to fly in it to our East European destination – headquarters of the airline to which it belonged. As we reached the foot of the ramp, an official stopped us and allowed only the first passenger to board. When sure that this one was actually in and seated, he allowed the second up the ramp. Only when the second was seated did he let the third aboard. It was a curious and interminably slow way of filling the plane. Being the last in line and waiting for the penultimate passenger to get to his seat, I asked the man at the ramp what it all meant.

'Quite simple,' he explained pleasantly and politely, 'if all the passengers crowded into the back entrance of the plane, it would tip up on to its tail!'

I smiled as pleasantly as I could to someone who expected me to believe such a ridiculous story, and then it was my turn to board.

Once airborne, I asked a stewardess the same question. She came up with the same answer. They're all mad, I thought, or they think I'm stupid! I was even more convinced of this when on arrival at our destination everyone made a mad scramble for the back exit. No one called them back to disembark singly, and the plane didn't tip up on its tail.

Again I was the last of the crowd and, as I walked down the ramp, I couldn't resist sneaking a look sideways at the tail which should have tipped up. Suddenly I stopped in mid-step, did a double-take and stared. There, underneath the tail, was a fork-top prop holding it up. One of the ground crew was standing by making sure it was doing its duty. This strange device was obviously peculiar to the home airport and not a regular piece of equipment to be found on West European fields.

'Why the prop?' I asked unbelievingly of the man at the foot of the ramp.

'Oh,' he explained brightly, 'if we didn't put that there the moment the plane comes to a halt, the weight of the passengers would make it . . .'

'. . . tip up on its tail!' I said, finishing the sentence with him.

Quite frankly, I have been less concerned about crashing in Eastern Europe than I have about getting food poisoning from the meals served on some planes. On one, I am sure that the adverse effects of inadvertently eating half a piece of mildewed fruit cake were only neutralised by downing big gulps of thick, black coffee which I would have otherwise avoided. Another airline served me a concoction claimed to be tea in a greasy tin mug. Some use plastic spoons which disintegrate in hot liquid . . . a little trick they may have learned from British Rail.

During one meal on Balkan Airlines, we were pleased to be given clean, if well-worn, stainless steel implements.

Closer examination of markings on these revealed that the knife had originated with LOT (Polish) Airlines, the fork had come from UNITED ARAB AIRLINES, a smaller butter knife was from SABENA and, just to make us feel at home, there was a BEA spoon! Somehow they had managed to get some butter marked MALEV (Hungarian airline), and only the inscription on the paper serviette reminded us of the airline on which we were actually flying.

Before I am accused of knocking Balkan Airlines, let me be fair and record that they do have just cause to claim one lead over every other airline I've ever flown. One morning when the peace-loving workers were slogging away to build their socialist paradise below, we bloated plutocrats were being served breakfast high above the clouds. And, unbelievably, the beverage with breakfast was a tumbler of champagne! The stewardess couldn't believe it when I declined such a generous serving of this truly capitalist drink.

I can never decide which is worse — the frightening experiences of travelling on East European airlines or the frustration of being grounded in some Communist capital without a serviceable aircraft in sight. Delayed flights are so common that I know every nook and cranny of most major East European airport departure lounges. Frustration is increased by the fact that in a censored society the most inspiring English newspaper available is usually an outdated copy of the 'Morning Star'. Having read their latest deficit, accompanied by strong urging of comrades to chip in, the delayed traveller is reduced to reading airline house journals. These are more entertaining than they sound, but whether it's the quaint English or political overtones that make them so, I'm never sure.

Consider this: 'The first freedom fighters from Bangladesh left for home on a charter aircraft of the INTERFLUG from Berlin-Schonefeld Central Airport in March after having been healed.'

The inauguration of flights between East Germany and Copenhagen gave INTERFLUG's magazine a logical reason to run a travel feature about the Danish capital. Pensiveness, politics and pride mingle unmistakeably in the climactic paragraphs of this piece of deathless prose. . . .

'After an extended stroll through the city our last visit is to the trade representation of the German Democratic Republic in the Svanemollevej 48. A bit of home in a distant country. A sign that the interest in Denmark in trade with our peace-loving socialist country is becoming ever greater.

'Night embraces the airport in Copenhagen-Kastrup. The TU 134 of the INTERFLUG is standing amidst the SAS machines, a symbol of the peaceful relations among the peoples.'

After sitting in Prague Airport through a long series of delayed departure announcements, the voice of harsh reality interrupted soothing background music which plays through the sound system between-times: 'We regret to inform the passengers of Flight so-and-so (my flight!) that the aircraft cannot be made serviceable and the flight is cancelled.'

The trauma of being told the awful truth had just reached its climax when the sound system resumed its music with the familiar voice of the friend who wrote the Foreword to this book. . . .

'When shall we meet again . . . ' the dulcet sound wafted across the huge departure hall.

'When indeed, Mr Richard!' I muttered as I tried to mentally revise my shattered schedule.

According to TIME Magazine, 'Flying in Eastern Europe . . . requires infinite patience and a certain sense of derring-do.' It's correspondent William Mader, a veteran of the Communist bloc airways, offered this advice: "Fly Eastern European only when there is no choice. . . . Plan appointments no earlier than 24 hours after scheduled arrival. Obtain transit visas, if possible, for all Eastern European countries in the flight pattern in case the flight is diverted. Steel nerves for a rough ride, regardless of weather. Be armed with plenty of Western reading material, for only in Yugoslavia can you buy it freely. If plane is diverted, immediately upon landing rush to transit counter and start demanding whatever other transportation is available. It will take hours to gain results. If not in a hurry, try to find the most comfortable chair, settle in for a long stay and relax."'

Worse than being delayed is arriving at the airport to be told that your booked and confirmed seat is not now available. This has only ever happened to me in Eastern Europe. Whether they overbook for the number of seats on the plane, or if they give preference to late-booking Party officials I have no idea. The fact remains that on one memorable occasion it looked as if two of us were to be stranded in an East European capital. This was doubly inconvenient because we had to be in Frankfurt for a committee meeting that evening.

Our stay in the East European city had been short. I had brought a few gifts for friends there . . . the kind of little things they find hard to get. For instance, one had asked me if I could bring a pair of nylon tights for his daughter-in-law, so I had fulfilled the request by bringing three or four cellophane packets of the hard-to-acquire items. What I didn't realise was that when fishing them out of my raincoat pocket, one packet remained lodged there. I didn't discover it until, at the airline check-in counter, I was told there were no seats left on the flight to Frankfurt. In an attitude of despair, I thrust my hands in my pockets thinking, 'What happens now?'

'But our seats are confirmed,' I pleaded with the check-in girl.

'I'm sorry,' she said, 'we have a full quota of passengers.'

'Then someone has our seats,' I protested.

Her reply was lost to me because at that precise moment my hand felt cellophane. Surprised, I pulled the packet from my pocket realising that it was now too late to get this extra pair to my friend for his daughter-in-law. But the girl behind the desk saw what I was holding and gazed at the packet with the deference reserved for something as desirable but as difficult to get as the Crown Jewels.

The things were no good to me so, with no ulterior motive whatever, I said: 'Would these be of any use to you?'

She grabbed them appreciatively and asked: 'What flight did you say?'

'Frankfurt,' I replied surprised, 'but . . . '

She was gone, and when she returned she announced: 'You're on it!'

When she gave us the boarding passes I was still trying to decide whether the incident was Divine direction or a fabulous fluke. Certainly it wasn't a premeditated tactic.

If my general impression of Eastern Europe's airlines is less than the best, I should be fair enough to balance the picture with the viewpoint of a fully satisfied customer. It comes from one Y. S. Romaya, an Iraqi importer and manufacturers' representative, whose unsolicited letter seems to endorse the 'charms and complaisance' INTERFLUG claim as characteristics of their stewardesses. A facsimile of his rather erratically typed letter appeared in the company's magazine exactly as follows: 'We beg also to state, that inspite, we are visiting Europe for the past several years with other airlines, but we should confess and declare that our trip ex Berlin to Beyrouth & Baghdad by Interflug, were very pleasant, seats were comfortable, very excellent food were rendered in addition to several services rendered to all passengers by stewards & hostesses which could not be forgotten.'

Well, if Y. S. Romaya was so impressed, who am I to complain?

Chapter Thirteen

HIGH-FLYING FEMALES

Airlines are run by women. It's true that faceless executives and administrative personnel may claim a male majority, but the average air traveller sees a female image. It's true that a few men have invaded the predominantly female domain of check-in counters, particularly in the United States, but the majority of those who take care of the customer's first physical contact with the company are girls.

In the air, it may be argued, the most important person aboard the plane is the captain . . . *always* a man. But to me the captain is usually no more than a disembodied voice crackling through an often inadequate amplification system to tell me that if I look out the left side I'll see we're flying over Paris. (That's always when I am sitting on the right side of the plane. If I happen to be on the left side, it's always cloudy.) But the people who really take care of me are the stewardesses. Again there is such a species as a male steward, but they are always outnumbered by the stewardesses aboard and they always strike me as men who missed their real calling. I can never help wondering if some of them were potential pilots who failed their finals!

To the casual observer, the life of an airline stewardess appears glamorous and fun-filled. The constant traveller knows better. These girls are work-horses expected to check and demonstrate safety devices, see that passengers have their seat belts fastened, pass out newspapers, make announcements, serve food and drink (sometimes at breakneck speed), be at the constant beck and call of a planeload of passengers and take care of special needs like the disposal of air-sickness bags and disposable baby whatsits! Then there are the unexpected crises like the tap in the toilet which refuses to shut off . . . or the character with the gun who insists on going to Cuba.

What about the privilege of going to so many places as part of the job? For most European stewardesses, the working day ends in exactly the same place it started. While they may have flown to Frankfurt, they saw only the inside of the airport before flying back again on the same aircraft. For those who fly further and get night stops, the faraway destination is probably no more to them than an airport, a road to town and the inside of a hotel room where they sink exhausted into bed after making sure to book their early call for tomorrow's flight home.

Working hours can be exhausting. Time changes traumatic. Such things as 'stand-bys' can be frustrating when it's a great day to go out but regulations require her to stay close enough to a particular phone to be summoned at a moment's notice for a flight to the other side of the Continent.

But for all this, most stewardesses enjoy their jobs. They are the kind of girls for whom a nine-to-five office routine would be sheer drudgery. They enjoy the variety in their job, and the different – even difficult – people they meet. And, apart from such exceptions as five-hour flights with few people aboard, they rarely suffer from boredom.

Stewardesses are usually attractive young ladies, but only in the United States has a conscious effort been made to turn them into sex symbols. In constant competition for customers some U.S. domestic lines have provided their girls with hot pants uniforms, and one line had its stewardesses changing outfits during flights in a sort of airborne fashion show! Another airline supplemented its usual contingent of stewardesses with Playboy 'bunnies' on one route where businessmen have a choice of airline.

But the majority of stewardesses project a different image. Attractive but modest. Capable. Intelligent. Friendly in a wholesome way. They vary slightly according to their nationality. European stewardesses are generally demure, friendly and efficient, whereas their American counterparts are talkative, friendly but slightly less efficient. While there are exceptions to every rule, I find that British stewardesses are a breed apart. While the majority of them are still as friendly and competent in their own way, whenever I meet the exception of an aloof, supercilious stewardess with a big superiority complex, she always seems to be British!

As I walked aboard one BEA Trident at Heathrow, I noticed the trolley of evening newspapers which would be distributed to passengers. Being in that category and happy to ease the load of the stewardess by helping myself, I was in the process of picking up an *Evening Standard* when a reproving voice boomed: 'One moment sir!'

The paper was snatched back and smartly replaced in the rack.

'But . . . ' I began, rather like a naughty schoolboy.

'If you will kindly take your seat sir,' she interrupted, 'we will bring the newspapers to you.'

Somewhat chastened, I went to a seat and strapped myself in.

Halfway to Geneva it suddenly occurred to me that the promised paper had never materialised. I stopped the stewardess on her next trip through the cabin and, rather apologetically, reminded her that I would like to have a newspaper.

'One moment sir,' she said in less-than-pleasant tones.

That moment and several more passed before we touched down at our destination. I left the plane, still not having had the newspaper.

American stewardesses tend toward the other extreme. Boarding a flight from Los Angeles to Philadelphia, I was greeted by: 'Hi there! I'm Jill. What's your name?' Admittedly there were less than a dozen passengers on the flight, but Jill was soon on first-name terms with most of them. When it was time for a hot meal to be served, there was a choice of three main courses. I chose. Jill frowned.

'It's not as good as it sounds,' she whispered confidentially.

I ordered according to her advice.

A few moments later she was taking a tray with my initial choice to a passenger in the First Class section. She stopped by my seat and lowered the tray.

'See what I mean?' she asked.

It did look unappetising. As she disappeared I wondered why the unsuspecting fellow up front hadn't been given the benefit of Jill's counsel when he ordered.

Suddenly she reappeared looking excited.

'Ever seen anything like that?' she asked, handing me something.

Until I was actually holding the object I had no idea what she was showing me. After all, it was the first time I had ever actually *handled* a glass eye!

'It belongs to a fellah up in First Class,' she informed me. 'Isn't it *good*!'

My mind conjured up hideous visions of a First Class passenger with an empty eye socket while Jill was showing me what should be in it.

'It's all right,' she said, as if sensing my disquiet, 'he has another one.'

For a brief moment I had visions of a blind man with *two* glass eyes before being assured that his other one was a replacement for the one I was holding.

'It's very realistic,' I conceded unenthusiastically.

'Not half as good as the new one!' enthused Jill. 'The

new one moves like the good one and even looks blood-shot!'

Just as I was wondering how long we were going to be discussing a fellow passenger's glass eye, Jill said: 'Here, give me the eye and I'll get you your lunch.'

If airline stewards give me the impression of failed pilots, some girls on ground-staff make me think of stewardesses who never quite made it. Whereas the average stewardess exudes an air of class and confidence, her ground-bound counterpart obviously gets worn down by the tedium of being tied to a desk.

The attractive young lady in uniform was framed by the front of the Information Desk in the pre-Customs area of Heathrow's Terminal Two. Having just arrived from Geneva, I was about to settle down and wait for my baggage when I saw her doing nothing and decided I could more usefully occupy my time and relieve her boredom.

'I need to book a seat on the next available flight to Belfast,' I told her.

'Can't do it here,' she said.

'No, I realise I can't buy a ticket here,' I explained, 'I am already holding an open ticket and all I need to do is reserve a seat.'

I glanced at the telephone alongside her, expecting her to pick it up and do the necessary.

'Can't do it here,' she repeated. 'You'll have to go to Terminal One.'

Well, she was labelled 'Information' so who was I to expect more from her? But at least I can check with her the *time* of the next flight to Belfast, I thought.

'Do you have a BEA timetable?' I asked.

'Sorry, we're out of them,' she replied.

I began to doubt the validity of the claim that this unhelpful soul was set up as a source of information. Then I noticed she had a flight list on the desk in front of her.

'Do you have Belfast flights listed there?' I asked hopefully.

'No,' she said.

Waves of frustration threatened to overwhelm me. Take it easy, I thought. Calm down. Think logically. What is the one item without which no airport information desk is complete, anywhere in the world? Of course! The ABC World Airways Guide in which all flights are listed and without which any self-respecting information girl would be lost.

'You have an ABC,' I said, more as a confident statement of fact than a query.

'No,' she said again.

But happily, the lack of this essential commodity finally stung her out of her lethargy. She actually picked up the telephone alongside her and obtained the information I needed.

One check-in girl who deserves a bouquet was sitting out a lonely vigil in the deserted departure area of a certain European airport when I came rushing in. On this occasion I was convinced I had missed my plane on which I was to fly to England. Not only was it past check-in time, but it was also five minutes after actual take-off time when the car in which I was travelling came screaming into the airport. The driver, my host, said it was worth a try in case the plane was delayed.

Rushing up to the desk, I pushed my ticket across the counter to this very young and, I think, inexperienced check-in girl.

'You're late,' she observed in neutral tones.

'I know,' I said, 'but has the plane actually left . . . or is it delayed?'

'It was delayed five minutes,' she replied, 'but now it's closed up and ready to taxi. You can't possibly make it.'

I was resigned to my fate of staying another night. It was my own fault. She was not to blame, but I thought

I could at least show her how lighthearted I was about the whole affair.

'You know,' I grinned, 'I thought you could take care of a VIP passenger better than that!'

She looked up startled, and grabbed my ticket again.

'One moment sir,' she said, dashing off like a scalded cat.

I wondered if she had taken me seriously, and my suspicions were confirmed when she reappeared with an important-looking gold braided official and a posse of porters. Two grabbed my cases. Another snatched my hand baggage. Before a fourth porter could pick *me* up, I took off after the frantically beckoning and profusely apologising official. Outside on the tarmac, the plane had been summoned back from beginning its taxiing. A ramp was being rushed up to it and the door swung open. Two smartly-uniformed stewardesses stepped out on to the top of the ramp and stood on either side of the door. (I had a horrible feeling they might even snap to attention and salute me as I dashed inside!)

Once seated and strapped in for take-off, I noticed them giving me sidelong glances. Obviously they were puzzled. As soon as the seat belt sign was switched off, one came over and ventured: 'Excuse me sir, but should we know you?'

As tactfully as possible I told her the truth, risking the possibility of being thrown out of the plane at thirty thousand feet. When I finished, there was a moment of stunned silence, and then she roared with laughter. Quickly she told her colleague and then, ignoring my protests, they went and told the pilot. Fortunately he was a friendly person and said something like 'anyone who pulls that kind of trick must be someone special'!

As air travel in Western Europe becomes more and more crowded, airports tend to develop into mere people processing plants. Everything becomes very impersonal. Often when crushed into an airport bus I dream of the seemingly unattainable . . . a private jet where I am the only passenger. The nearest I got to this was when I found myself alone in the departure lounge of an American airport.

'Where are the other passengers?' I asked an official, as much to confirm I was in the right place as to get an answer to my question.

'They'll be coming,' he assured me, and disappeared.

The final minutes to flight time ticked by. I was still alone. The plane stood like a sentinel outside, looking as lonely as I felt. Elsewhere in the airport crowds of passengers jostled their way to other departure lounges for other flights. Finally, a stewardess appeared in the doorway of the plane outside. Looking puzzled, she came down the ramp and into the departure lounge.

'Where's everyone?' she asked.

'I was about to ask you the same question,' I replied.

'You'd better get aboard while I find out what's happening,' she instructed, picking up a nearby telephone.

I boarded the plane and exercised the rare privilege of choosing whichever seat I preferred. A few moments later, the stewardess returned.

'Funny,' she said, 'they don't seem to have anyone else for this flight.'

She closed the plane door and walked toward the back of the aircraft. Engines sprang to life, and soon we were taxiing toward the end of the runway. It was a strange feeling. There I was sitting in solitary state while the only other passenger cabin occupant – my very own personal stewardess – was reaching for the microphone to make the customary announcement.

'Ladies and gentleman,' she began. 'Welcome to our flight number . . . '

And then she stopped. She coughed slightly, and started again.

'Sir, we welcome you aboard . . . '

She stopped again, and by this time we were airborne.

'Aw, hang it,' I heard her mutter embarrassedly. Then she hung up her microphone, marched down the long empty centre aisle to the only occupied seat in the entire aircraft, and suggested: 'How about you and me having coffee?'

Chapter Fourteen

DRIVING HAZARDS

I am fully qualified as a car driver in Britain, Switzerland and the United States. With those licences I can drive anywhere in the world. Britain has a driving test which many first-timers fail. Switzerland demands a full-scale written test before the would-be driver is put through a road test stringent enough to reduce any but the ultra-confident to a quivering mass. And in the State from which I got my transatlantic license (they spell it with an 's' there!) it is required to have a written test, road test *and* an eye test.

I never failed to obtain any of these licences, probably because I never completed the tests. The story of how I got three licences with few of the irritating formalities accompanying them begins in a Continental country which had better be nameless. It was there that my collection of qualifications began with an *international* driver's licence! The saga started in a busy European city one day when the Continental friend with whom I was working handed me the keys of his car.

'I don't drive,' I said apologetically.

'You don't drive!' he exclaimed in disbelief. 'You travel so much and you don't drive!'

'I use trains, buses, boats, planes . . . and other people's cars when they are driving them,' I explained, 'but I don't own a car myself, and I don't have a licence to drive.'

'But surely you know *how* to drive a car,' he persisted.

'Oh yes,' I admitted, 'but it's no use giving me your

keys because I don't have a licence.'

He agreed rather glumly, and then brightened.

'We'll get you a licence!' he announced.

'But how?'

'Come with me.'

We drove (or rather he drove us) into town where we parked and went into an office.

'My friend needs a licence,' he announced, and papers were produced for me to complete.

'But I don't really need one of your licences,' I protested.

'You're not getting one,' he said. 'These papers are for an international licence. You want to drive in other countries as well, don't you?'

I gaped.

'What do I have to do for this?' I asked.

'Pay a fee,' he said, mentioning a very modest amount.

'. . . and give us two pictures of yourself, one for our files and one for your licence,' added the man who had produced the papers.

'But I don't have two pictures of myself,' I said, thinking I had found a way of escape.

'No pictures?' asked the man.

'No,' I said, pulling out my wallet and opening it as if to endorse the point. A dog-eared polyfoto fell out.

'Here's a picture!' said the man, picking it up. I had forgotten it was there.

'But only one,' I said, still feeling I was ahead of him.

'That's all right,' he allowed, 'we don't really need one for our files.'

'But what about a test?' I insisted.

'Can't you drive?' he asked.

'Well, yes,' I said dubiously.

'Fine!' he said, 'then all you need to do is complete the form.'

'But I don't have a licence already,' I pointed out, feeling that some kind of national endorsement of my driving capability should be a prerequisite to my being let loose on the roads of the rest of the world.

'Of course you don't have a licence,' he agreed, 'otherwise you wouldn't be applying for one.'

I might add at this point that the country concerned later fell in line with every other country of Europe and introduced driving tests for their own nationals and the requirement of a national driver's licence before issuing the international document. My first accident may have prompted them to change their over-the-counter, no-questions-asked method of issuing licences!

I walked from the office a 'fully-qualified' driver with an impressive-looking licence of many pages in a variety of languages.

Travelling to the United States, I decided I would get an American licence which would be more convincing than the easily-obtained document already in my possession.

The man in the appropriate office asked me if I had any kind of licence. He seemed more impressed than I with the one I produced.

'In that case,' he said, 'we can dispense with the road test if you promise one thing.'

'What's that?' I asked.

He glanced at my British passport, and said: 'Drive on the *right* side of the road!'

This is stupid, I thought, as I returned to England. I now had two driver's licences, neither of which was British.

The British official listened to my request.

'Do you have a licence at present?' he asked.

'Yes,' I said, producing the American one.

'In that case you're experienced enough to forego a full-scale test if you can go through the motions.'

Having just driven around the United States, I didn't suggest I needed more.

When we arrived in Switzerland, a British friend warned me that the Swiss would demand I take a test. And, he added, the test was so stiff and his wife had failed it so many times that she decided to give up driving!

My other licences would see me through only until I was recognised as an official resident, but really it was a matter of putting off the evil day. I heard about the written test which demanded almost completely memorised knowledge of a thick paperback book of rules. These included regulations concerning huge lorries which I would never need to know. And the road test! Not just along normal roads through the usual traffic, I was told, but over a specially-prepared course in a private testing area. The description sounded like an advanced driver's nightmare or a qualification run for the Grand Prix! I was petrified!

Then, suddenly and without warning, the Swiss changed their laws just in time. I would still need to obtain a Swiss licence, but this would be issued immediately on production of a valid British or American liecnce. I produced both as if to speed its issue before they changed their minds!

My wife, a non-driver before coming to Switzerland, took her written test without formal instruction. A useless thing to attempt, according to her driving instructor who claimed he had seen no one pass it without a series of expensive classroom lessons. She succeeded first time, qualifying to take the tough practical test. Her first attempt at that was equally successful. The only difference between her Swiss licence and mine is that she really deserves hers!

There are few ways of cutting the basic cost of travelling by car, but there is ample opportunity to increase it by inadvertently breaking traffic regulations in unfamiliar areas. The avoidance of fines is therefore a point of economy, but it can be difficult sometimes.

In one East European country I was following a huge lorry for ages when we finally reached a stretch of straight road. Overtaking was simple because nothing was coming in the opposite direction, but as I regained my side of the road I saw a police car in a lay-by ahead. He flagged me down. Writing a ticket, he said he was fining me for overtaking.

'But there's nothing to say it's forbidden,' I protested.

He agreed that there was no actual sign, but pointed to the road. I looked at the wet surface where winter snows had recently melted. There wasn't a line of any kind on the road, double or single, continuous or broken.

'Before the snow and ice removed them,' indicated the policeman, 'there were double lines there, and you must not cross them.'

'I know the regulations about double lines,' I said. 'I never cross them, and since there are none there now I still haven't. I have never driven down this road before. Overtaking was perfectly safe. I did not know there should be double lines there and how could I be expected to guess that the snow washed them away?'

'Passport,' he demanded gruffly.

He just wants to prove I'm a stupid foreigner before letting me off, I thought, so I produced my passport. He didn't even open it, but quickly stuffed it inside his tunic.

'You get passport when you pay fine,' he said, with the air of a safe-cracker who's found the combination.

I had no alternative. The fine was small. The principle was big. I still seethe when I think of it.

I should have remembered the passport trick. It was played on us in the same East European country years before when a friend of mine was driving. This time it was a 'speed trap' operated on a remote, long and straight road miles from any built up area. The trap consisted of a lone policeman who, I swear, had propped a portable speed limit sign in the hedge (half obscured by shrubbery) and then dashed off down the road to flag down passing cars and collect fines. He had no way of measuring speed, and only a bicycle to chase them if they refused to stop!

After effectively pulling the passport trick, he sent us

on our way fuming. Some miles on, when we were nearing a large city, a couple of policemen with a car alongside them leapt out to stop us.

'Not again!' said my friend, putting his foot on the accelerator and roaring through the 'roadblock'.

I was horrified!

'They had a car,' I said, 'they'll be after us!'

'I think they are,' he answered, glancing in his mirror and pressing the accelerator to the floor boards.

Visions of languishing in an East European gaol loomed before me. I glanced behind. The following car was keeping pace with our breakneck speed, but not yet decreasing the distance between us. It didn't encourage me because we were just entering the city and couldn't possibly maintain our present speed. And visions of jumping red lights and complicating our already precarious position in the eyes of the law made me feel sick.

'As soon as we hit traffic, we'll abandon ship,' my friend instructed, leaving much to be desired in his choice of verbs.

'All right,' I agreed gloomily, glancing back and seeing the car still following.

We roared into a square, made a sharp right and straight into the parking space in front of a hotel.

'Everybody out,' yelled my friend, and the two of us just managed to get through the glass doors of the hotel lobby before our pursuers' car arrived and, instead of roaring past as we hoped, came screeching to a halt alongside ours.

My visions of our imminent arrest became muddled as two people in plain clothes leapt from the car and dashed in our direction.

'But that's not a police car . . . ' I was beginning to say as I recognised a British make and licence plate.

The two strangers burst into the hotel lobby and said excitedly: 'We saw what you did at that roadblock. We were behind you, so we did the same thing!'

None of us need have worried. There wasn't a police car in sight.

Driving in Eastern Europe has unexpected hazards. Once off main highways, any subsidiary roads which are surfaced tend to deteriorate into pot holes. In really rural areas, they wind up as dirt tracks. They may still be negotiable in normal circumstances, give or take some wear and tear on springs and shock absorbers, but when heavy rains come its best to give up and go home.

Caught in such rain on one occasion, I was reluctant to proceed with my brand new stationwagon. Water was already ankle-deep and we were only maintaining an even keel because the car was fully-loaded with people and equipment.

'It's only across the river now,' said my interpreter who was one of the people travelling with Susan and me to our scheduled meeting.

'Over there,' he pointed across a swirling, swollen river alongside which we were driving. I could see silhouettes of buildings on the opposite side, and a few flickering lights. Electricity, such as it was, had long since failed.

'There's the bridge!' he exclaimed as it appeared to our right just ahead.

As I made the ninety-degree turn to drive on to it, I had second thoughts. When the headlights illuminated it, I realised that all I could see of the structure was wooden handrails on each side. The actual surface over which we were to drive was already submerged beneath the fast-flowing river. The water was rushing through the skinny handrails as if they didn't exist.

'It's not too deep,' said someone, indicating the water swirling across the bridge. 'Look, there are men standing on it!'

Sure enough there were. All were standing on the upstream side leaning over the handrail holding long sticks in the water.

They can't be fishing, I thought! But what in the world *are* they doing standing there in the darkness during a raging storm with drenching rain? The nearest one looked toward our headlights and beckoned me on to the bridge. I saw that the water was only up to his ankles, so I assumed we could make it.

Was it the rushing water, the deluge of rain, a clap of thunder or a streak of lightning which gave me the distinct impression of the wooden bridge actually swaying as the loaded car inched across it?

Once on the other side, we stopped. Villagers rushed through the rain to meet us. The men on the bridge remained in position, and I had noticed a curious thing as we had passed them. They were roped together.

'What are those men doing?' we asked one of the villagers.

'The wooden bridge is not strong,' they explained. The rushing water weakens it still further. Any additional strain could be disastrous. The men station themselves on the bridge with sticks to break the impact of any large logs or tree trunks rushing down with the water. If one were to hit with force, the bridge would certainly collapse!'

When the meeting was over, the bridge was still standing. But we drove off another way!

Often I am asked where, of all the countries in which I drive, do I find the worst drivers. Unhappily, I must confess that they are undoubtedly in one of my favourite lands . . . Israel. I love the Jewish people deeply, but I hate their driving fervently. I could happily live in the exciting land of Israel, and even die there. And when I drive a car in Jerusalem, I'm convinced I will!

American drivers can be rated as among the best in the world. There's a rotten apple in every barrel, but generally I find the average American to be careful, thoughtful and courteous behind the wheel. He is short on sympathy for the stupidity of others. I know one American who carries a bunch of things which look like parking tickets when placed beneath the windscreen wiper of a selfish or stupid parker. After giving him a slight shock before he discovers it isn't official, it subjects the offender to a stream of belittling abuse about his inability to park a car in a way which will not inconvenience others, and goes on to wish him early transmission failure 'preferably on the expressway at 4 a.m.' and concludes wishing that 'the fleas of a thousand camels will infest your armpits'!

My acquaintance is a highly-respected and otherwise tolerant Christian businessman. But, as I say, the American driver who maintains a high standard expects others to match it!

In Europe, different nationalities have different motoring idiosyncracies, shortcomings and irritating driving habits. Only the Italians can claim monopoly on all of them! One travel writer gives this advice to those planning to drive in Italy. . . .

'There is a simple method of achieving the right state of mind for driving in Italy. Before you start your car for the first time, sit in the driver's seat, hold the steering-wheel and think the following: *I am the only driver on the road, and mine is the only car*. It may be hard to believe, especially after you have seen Rome during the first week of July or Milan during the rush hour, but millions of Italian drivers believe it and so can you. An Italian driver's reaction to any encounter with another vehicle is, first, stunned disbelief, then outrage. You don't have a chance unless you can match this faith. It isn't enough to say you are the only driver, or to think it – you've got to believe it. Remember, your car is THE CAR; all others are aberrations in the divine scheme.'

France has its 'weekend' drivers who subscribe to a system of insurance which doesn't cover them on working days. This is a fine money-saving device for those whose cars stay in the garage all week, but it tends to make the roads even more crowded than usual at weekends.

Spanish motoring tends to become more hazardous than usual during the hours of twilight. This is the time when many farmers are heading for home along rural roads in donkey carts. The cart carries no lights, and the only human occupant is usually asleep in the back.

Most accidents in Spain are dealt with quite simply. The offending driver is thrown in jail. Explanations come later.

'Priority to the right' is a Continental ruling which baffles British drivers, and many of them come home with dents down the right side of their cars to prove it! The thing is quite simple. If you're driving into a main road from the right and there is no sign to stop or yield right of way, just hurtle into the fast-moving traffic with complete abandon. There is the possibility of getting yourself killed, but you can die knowing that you were legally correct. If you are driving along a main road, just view every road on the right with suspicion! Even if there is a stop sign for the incoming driver, he will often thrust his vehicle into the traffic as far as he dares.

The British driver dare not condemn Continentals when he indulges in his own peculiar sins, the cardinal one being dawdling in the fast lane of the M4 impervious to the mute pleas of the headlight flasher leading the line of traffic behind.

Chapter Fifteen

INTERNATIONAL MAN

Travelling has bestowed on me something of an international character. My basic appearance, which some find difficult to define in terms of origin, also has something to do with it.

In Spain, they accept me as one of their own. Italians give me sort of 'is-he-or-isn't-he?' glances. In another country, I was making a telephone call from the reception desk of a hotel when someone who didn't speak English answered the telephone. I handed the receiver to the receptionist with the request that she interpret.

'Here was I thinking how marvellous your English was,' she commented afterwards, 'because I thought we shared the same mother tongue!'

In Israel, a government official scratched his head and said: 'You're the most Jewish Gentile I've ever met!'

But one airline security man treated me with the kind of suspicion such gentlemen reserve for Arabs.

The most common error is for new acquaintances to mistake me for an American. With an accent which once betrayed my Westcountry origins but is now so polluted as to be termed by someone 'international English,' I am constantly called on to satisfy curiosity. My wife, whose early elocution training was with the view to becoming a Shakespearean actress, raises no such questions.

I was born just one mile from where the Pilgrim Fathers set sail at Plymouth. Mine missed the boat.

Following those early settlers many years later, I discovered I could fit into the American scene like a hand in a glove. They pronounced the word 'half' more as 'haf' than 'hof', in the same way as my fellow Westcountrymen. They roll their r's similarly. In fact, one or two Americans of my acquantance could easily pass as having come from the West of England. Now, having visited the United States on countless occasions, it is very hard to believe that there was ever a first time. On the other hand, driving 7,000 miles on what was then 'the wrong side of the road' for me, is an experience I'll never forget.

The first American car to fall into my very young and inexperienced hands was a 1952 Oldsmobile. I got it cheap, and understood why within the first hundred miles. Its automatic transmission failed.

The thought of driving on the right side of the road when all my experience had been on the left didn't bother me half as much as the awkward feeling of a left-hand drive. (I now feel just as awkward during the first couple of miles in a right-hand drive car.) And without a clutch to caress, my left foot seemed like so much excess baggage. I wanted to drape it out the window.

To the car dealer's assurances of 'gotta good buy there', I coasted the car down a slight incline from the parking lot to a filling station next door. I was thankful this did not necessitate venturing out into the roaring bumper-to-bumper traffic of the eight-lane highway which was to be my next test of confidence.

'Fill her up!' I called to the attendant, who looked at me strangely. Suddenly I realised I had parked on the wrong side of the pump.

'I'm sorry,' I explained embarrassedly, 'I'm from the other side of the Atlantic where they build cars the other way 'round!'

He squinted at me strangely. He was a simple, provincial soul who had never heard of the idiosyncracies of British motoring.

'No kidding!' he exclaimed, as impressed as if he had just encountered someone from the other side of the moon.

I was out of the car, considering the major task of getting it to the other side of the pump. It was my first 'automatic' car and I was wondering how to put the wretched thing in reverse.

'It's all right,' he said, to my relief, 'I can reach across.'

He dragged the pump pipe across the car and proceeded to fill it. 'Thanks,' I said, paying him, forgetfully getting into the right side of the car and wondering where the driving wheel had gone!

Quickly I slid across the bench seat before he noticed. Flustered by my mistake and reminding myself to drive on the *right* side of the road, I started fumbling for a gear stick which wasn't here, stamped my left foot to the floorboards where the clutch should have been and then tried to remind myself of the fact that this was automatic transmission.

I grinned stupidly at the attendant who was standing with a bemused look on his face as he watched my performance.

'You sure you can handle that thing?' he asked dubiously.

'Of course,' I replied with false confidence. 'It's just that cars are so different in Britain that it takes a little adjustment. You know, what you call a "hood" we call a "bonnet". And what you call a "trunk" is to us a "boot". We have "windscreens" instead of "windshields", and "wings" instead of "fenders" . . . '

My flood of words was to cover more than my embarrassment. Somehow I couldn't get this stupid car to move forward. Behind my diversionary explanations to the attendant, I was frantically reviewing the order of starting. The transmission was in DRIVE and the engine was running. Why then did this ridiculous vehicle fail to budge an inch?

As I ran out of explanations on the differences between British and American cars, the attendant bent down and pointed through my open window.

'In America,' he said, 'we call that thing a handbrake, and our cars go much better when you release it!'

Europe is now catching up to America's seemingly insuperable lead in road development, but to a pre-motorway Britisher the eight-lane super-highway on which I was forced to first drive that car was a nightmare. Getting on it was a major operation as traffic hurtled by thick and fast. Finally there was a gap. My mind was still not adjusted from gear shift to automatic and I finally shot the car out into the road with such ferocity that I thought an accident was inevitable. Mercifully it didn't happen because some sweet guardian angel had arranged the impossible of having the three lanes across which I shot entirely free of traffic at that particular moment.

I straightened the car in the direction of the traffic (which was exactly opposite to the way I wished to go, but there was nothing else for it) and hit the accelerator hard. The car roared and leapt forward like a scalded cat about to go into orbit. No one had told me that the completely depressed accelerator automatically activated a ferocious 'overtaking' gear.

Having avoided hitting the car in front, I addressed myself to the problem of going in the other direction before covering too many miles the wrong way. A U-turn was illegal, and impossible because of a central barrier. I would have to get off at a right exit, somehow cross over or under on a small road, and then head back in the right direction. Nothing could be simpler now but it was a major operation then. The car was controlling me rather than the other way around. I was clutching the wheel like the grim death I expected at any moment. I was driving too fast for comfort, but I had to observe a *minimum* speed limit which I had never encountered before. Worst of all, it became painfully obvious that, unlike in Europe, American drivers are permitted to pass on *either* side of the car ahead on a multi-lane highway. Being in a middle lane and sticking to it like a leech, cars were roaring past me on both sides. To crown my misery I discovered that the indicator wasn't functioning.

It took me twenty miles to escape. The car was still in one piece. I was a quivering nervous wreck.

It didn't take me long to get into the groove of American driving. Soon I was driving hundreds of miles a day without a care. My first American puncture introduced me to a jack which didn't work, but a helpful stranger came to assist me in changing the wheel for a perilously smooth spare. Since it was very late at night and I had only 20 miles of a tiring 500-mile journey to complete, I decided to press on carefully.

Two miles from my destination, it blew! There was nothing for it but to abandon ship. As I was locking the loaded vehicle another car drew alongside.

'Whadya dumpin' that there for?' asked the policeman driver.

I pointed to the disintegrated tyre and explained that until 18 miles back that had been my spare.

'Your car'll be busted and stripped if you leave it,' he assured me.

The problem was soon solved, but my host that night was horrified that I had considered leaving the car, even for a short time. Later I heard of a man in similar circumstances who walked to the nearest telephone to summon help. When he returned, he noticed another car pulled in, the driver of which had jacked up the back end of his incapacitated vehicle and was systematically stripping off various bits and pieces.

'Hey, wait a minute!' yelled the horrified motorist.

The newcomer looked out from under the back end unconcerned.

'Listen buddy,' he said, 'I found it first, but I'm only

interested in stuff from the back. You take anything you want from the front!'

American policemen have a tendency to be less polite than, say, their Swiss counterparts. The Swiss motorcycle cop will roar past a speeding motorist, flag him to the side, come back, salute, smile, comment on the weather and even shake hands before booking him. One, who was booking me for using snow tyres the day after Swiss authorities decree that snow will not fall, politely asked to borrow my pen to write the ticket!

The American, on the other hand, is more likely to dispense with formalities and open roadside proceedings with: 'O.K. buddy, let's see your pilot's licence!'

On one occasion, I was riding with a clergyman who was a qualified aviator. A policeman stopped us as we hurried to a meeting. He used the 'pilot's licence' line, so my friend handed him exactly what he asked for. The dumbfounded speed cop's face dropped.

'O.K. wise guy,' he said, handing it back, 'forget it this time but don't do it again.'

U.S. drivers' licences include more information about the holder than those in Europe. Mine included the colour of my eyes and hair, state of vision and many other details. One driver was stopped by a policeman who, on examining his licence, said: 'You should be wearing glasses.'

'I've got contacts,' explained the lens-wearer confidently.

'I don't care *who* you know,' screamed the lawman, 'you should be wearing glasses!'

Europeans tend to regard air conditioning in cars as a luxury, but in some parts of the States it is a necessity. Susan was with me driving through one very hot American summer. Our car windows were permananetly wound down, travel clothing was minimal and even this was loosened as soon as we got in the car.

On one occasion a massive, evil-looking insect flew in

through the open window and sat defiantly on the dashboard. Susan screamed and I swerved. Almost before the car came to a halt at the side of the road, we leapt out and promptly created another traffic hazard. Susan's skirt, unhooked for comfort while sitting in the car, slid gracefully to the ground!

One of my Continental cohorts now living in Britain told me of a similar experience on a German autobahn. Travelling with his wife and children, with a mountain of luggage on the roofrack, he glanced in his rearview mirror just in time to see one of his cases go flying off. Recognising the danger to both case and oncoming cars, he pulled over quickly, leapt out and began running back along the road. He, too, had not remembered his undone trouser belt until his wild dash was hopelessly delayed as his trousers descended to his ankles.

The fuel consumption of American cars tends to horrify Europeans. I once saw a cartoon showing a large American car in a filling station. The pump attendant was saying to the driver: 'Please switch off your engine sir, you're getting ahead of me.'

I thought that was funny until I had that Oldsmobile. It proved to be a good car in the end. It was capable of passing anything on the road except a filling station!

As sorry as I was to see it go, its fate was sealed by the fact that I needed the proceeds of the sale to cover the cost of my ticket back to Europe.

Chapter Sixteen

INTERNATIONAL RAIL

Trains were a form of travel I used more than anything else in my early days around Britain and the Continent. Whenever someone would meet me from a train, seeing the mountain of equipment I had with me, the invariable question was: 'Why don't you get a car?'

There were two answers to that question, and the second was that I couldn't afford it. But the equally truthful explanation I would share with those who enquired was that I never really minded train travel. I could work on the train, writing, editing, planning, preparing. Baggage travelled in the special van provided, and porters would handle it at stations. Generally it was less wearing than covering the same number of miles by car.

At that time British Rail fares were reasonable enough that passengers didn't need a bank loan to pay them, but my costs were always inflated because of my heavy equipment. This went through the ritual weighing and, according to the disposition of the man who calculated it, an excess baggage charge was imposed. It didn't take me long to discover that on my longer journeys the price of my excess baggage was more than the difference between Second and First Class fares. And since First Class passengers were granted an increased free baggage allowance large enough to include everything I carried, it was *cheaper* for me to 'go First'!

But whenever I did this, I'd nip smartly through to the Second Class section as the train arrived at my destination. Most of those who met me were habitual Second Class passengers who would find it difficult to understand – much less believe – my explanation that I could travel First Class cheaper!

Statistics prove that rail is one of the safest forms of travel but, curiously enough, it was in a railway station that my travel days may have ended. During a series of meetings in Kent, I had to return to my Eastbourne office for a meeting of our magazine's Editorial Board. To avoid a rather tedious train journey, my host kindly offered to drive me there, and get me back in time for the evening meeting. That day, two trains collided in Eastbourne Station. Five people were killed. I could have been one of them.

The British Rail Enquiry Office at Eastbourne was almost my second home when I was back in town. No sooner had I finished one tour than I'd be in there planning the next. While a procession of less complicated travellers dashed in and out to find the time of the next train to London, I'd be monopolising the entire services of one clerk for ages. Isolated at one end of a counter, we'd be poring over timetables with mutterings such as 'must be in Leeds by five . . . but surely this can be done without changing *twice* . . . isn't there *any* way of avoiding two hours stuck on Crewe Station?'

One day, while completely absorbed in our task, I had just mentioned the next stage of my journey when a familiar voice behind me suggested the train I needed to catch, where I had to change and the exact time of my arrival. As the enquiry clerk looked a little peeved at the interruption from a mere layman who couldn't possibly pour forth such complicated information without referring to a timetable, I greeted my good friend Eric Hutchings. Apart from his obvious calling as an evangelist, Eric has an uncanny memory for many things including scripture references and train times. He must find the former easier because they don't change with the seasons, but his competence with the latter was quickly endorsed by the astounded clerk who confirmed from the timetable that Eric's advice was completely accurate!

Since then I've often wondered if Dr Hutchings has ever mixed his memory systems while preaching to a vast crowd or speaking on radio. I visualise him quoting scripture and reference something like this: 'All have sinned, and come short of the glory of God" – Victoria 2:45'!

British Rail bears the brunt of many a barbed joke, but they served me reasonably well. Their timing didn't always tally with mine. But then, it rarely bore resemblance to that which they published, confidently and without shame, in their timetables! This was always accepted as one of the facts of life before I moved to Switzerland where I can usually set my very accurate Swiss watch by the time-keeping of the trains.

Continental railways have a lot in common, but they do have distinctive national and cultural characteristics from country to country. Generally they tend to deteriorate from north to south. Swedish trains are the last word in luxury and efficiency to which Italian rolling stock bears not the slightest resemblance. Latin travellers seem to have two things in common . . . mountains of baggage and plastic carrier bags filled with bottles of wine. If they don't have a gigantic compressed-cardboard suitcase which either falls off the rack or blocks the corridor, all their goods and chattels are bound up in a massive sheet. At meal times, which seem to last most of the journey, compartments are transformed into banqueting halls with salami sandwiches and juice-dripping oranges all over the place. The smell of garlic mingled with cheap cigarette smoke wafts through the corridors and every dull journey is changed into a convivial event.

Trains across Eastern Europe are something else. My most recent experience was made necessary by the cancellation of a plane. The only alternative was a 14-hour journey on the 'Istanbul Express'. To anyone thinking of riding this particular train, I would offer one word of advice . . . don't! Those who, like me, have no choice, should stock up with food sufficient for the entire trip. There is no restaurant car, not even a buffet. And those whose journey ends in Sofia should be warned that as they stagger, dazed and travel-worn, from the station they are likely to meet the biggest capitalists in Communist Bulgaria. Taxi drivers! In fact Britons who believe that inflated profits are made possible only by Conservative governments should consider the highway robberies these comrades carry out on unsuspecting tourists!

Many a night in Britain has been spent rumbling across the countryside in a railway sleeping compartment. Since I sleep like a log under any circumstances, this has always seemed an excellent way of saving both time and hotel bills. When I first ventured on to the Continent, longer distances made night travel inevitable. I had no reason to doubt that sleeping arrangements would be as civilised and respectable as in Britain. My first night ride across the Continent was an education.

I had never seen a sleeping compartment accommodating six people. Two had been the maximum. What's more, they didn't seem to share the British concern for segregating the sexes. My first such journey was shared by a married couple, two old ladies, an alcoholic farmworker and his dog.

To be fair, there seems to be an unwritten rule that occupants can only strip to underwear when of the same sex. Mixed compartments mean that only jackets and footwear can be decently disposed of. On one journey back from Spain, my wife and I shared a sleeping compartment with a rather rotund priest. He must have had dreams of being a deceased Pope lying in state because the way he slept matched such an image exactly. He felt able to remove his black saucer-like hat, but not his boots. He appeared to be stiffly at attention while flat on his back, his hat perched ludicrously on the bulge of his priestly stomach.

On one occasion I was quite sure I had an entire six-berth sleeping compartment to myself. But, soon after the train left the station, a couple who had been creating quite a commotion saying 'goodbye' to a host of friends finally found their way to 'my 'compartment. Young and well-dressed, they looked a little disappointed to see me at first. Then they brightened up, produced a bottle of champagne and a packet of plastic beakers.

'We have just been married,' they announced in broken English and, as the champagne cork exploded, 'will you help us to celebrate!'

I congratulated them . . . and fled!

One night I boarded a train after midnight. I had no reservation for a sleeping berth and, those who had were already safely tucked in them. Finding one of the attendants, I asked him if there any spare spaces. After paying him the appropriate fee, plus a tip, he led me to a compartment.

'Middle bunk on thc right,' he muttered, gently opening the door, 'and don't switch on the light or make a noise because everyone's already asleep.'

I complied and climbed into the bunk indicated. Gentle snores and heavy breathing indicated that fellow-occupants were, as he said, fast asleep.

The first thing I heard in the morning was a child crying below me, followed by an unmistakably feminine 'Sh-hh-sh!' The child persisted. The person I assumed was its mother sighed in a resigned kind of way, and I heard the bunk below creaking as she got out. Standing up, her back – mercifully – was only a couple of inches from my face when the awful realisation came over me like an icy wave. She was undressed.

As she fumbled for some kind of covering to make her decent enough to take her child on the now essential trip down the corridor, I was quietly slipping below my single blanket. I was scared that at any moment she would turn, see me and run out screaming.

She didn't and, as she disappeared out of the door my escape was already planned. I could nip out quickly while she was gone and the others still slept. The others! Another awful thought crossed my mind. If the person I had seen was female, and if she had felt free to shed her clothes the night before, every other sleeping body in that compartment must be of the same sex . . . and probably equally undressed!

Escape was now essential. I could hear screams ringing in my imagination. The concerned shouts of other passengers. Police. Prison. And bold headlines of the kind which would be echoed across the wires of international press agencies . . . 'EVANGELIST HELD ON CHARGES OF . . . ' The rest didn't bear thinking about.

I was just slipping surreptitiously from under my blanket when there was a movement from the upper bunk on the opposite side. She sat up and stretched to relieve the cramp of the confined quarters. I shot back under my blanket before she saw me.

That was it. I was trapped. Mother and child returned while Female No. 2 was dressing. Nearly suffocating under that bad-smelling blanket, I heard the rest of the sleepers were greeting the morn and each other. The whole compartment became a cacophony of foreign feminine chatter. I was so miserable.

The door was opening and closing. Trips were being made down the corridor, but never was I left completely alone. Fortunately none of them ventured to check on what they must have recognised as a 'sleeping' form completely covered by a blanket. Finally I felt the train come grinding to a halt, and heard excited voices indicating that this must be the end of the line. Baggage was being dragged around. The child was protesting. Farewells were being said, and then all sounds within the compartment subsided.

I waited a few moments before warily lifting the blanket. Unless one of them was still out of my vision in the bunk above me, they had all gone. I breathed a heavy sigh of relief as I looked around the deserted but obviously well-used compartment. Then I looked down to the floor, and froze! There, amid chocolate wrappings and orange peel was a pair of man's shoes. Mine. Hadn't they seen them? They couldn't have overlooked them! But no one had screamed. Perhaps they didn't care.

I pulled on my shoes and staggered into the deserted corridor. The carriage was empty except for the attendant just beginning to clean things up. He looked my way as I headed for the carriage door to the station platform.

'Have a comfortable night?' he asked, grinning.

It's a very long time since I rode a night train to any where on the Continent. But when the occasion arises again, I'll be very tempted to invest in the privacy of a First Class berth.

The memory I like most about train travel relates to an incident in Eastern Europe. Recording engineer Don Feltham and I were travelling between two major cities with a Christian friend . . . a national of that country. We had the compartment to ourselves and were enjoying the beautiful snow-covered countryside through which we were travelling.

Suddenly the ticket collector appeared and we began the usual fumble in our pockets. While this was going on our friend began chatting to him. We couldn't understand their conversation but it seemed to be good-natured and very ordinary chit chat.

'What were you telling him?' we asked casually when the ticket collector had gone.

'I was telling him how good it is to know Jesus,' was the reply.

It was beautiful. So natural. There had been no intense

questioning. No embarrassed silences. Nothing to convey to us that they had been engaged in anything more fantastic than discussing the weather. And yet in those few moments our friend had been sharing his faith with a man to whom the name of Jesus was very remote, to say the least.

The journey continued and, as we were nearing our destination, the ticket collector reappeared. This time he not only came into the compartment, but sat down by our friend showing an obvious eagerness as he said something.

Our friend turned to us and said in English: 'Excuse me a moment. He says he has now finished examining tickets. He wants me to tell him how he can know Jesus.'

Chapter Seventeen

ARE YOU CLIFF RICHARD?

The first time I flew anywhere with Cliff Richard, he forgot his passport. We were checking in at London Airport before he was hit by the awful realisation that this all-important document was sitting on his hall table at home.

At such times it is a definite asset to be a well-known personality. Our destination was Stockholm, and an SAS representative simply telexed the information to Arlanda Airport ahead of us. On arrival, sympathetic officials waved him through and the airline flew in his passport the following day enabling us to continue travelling without further complications.

If such an incident gives the impression of an inept traveller, nothing is further from the truth. Cliff is a veteran travelling man who has probably clocked up more miles than I have. He is the most placid and panic-free traveller I know. I have never heard him complain about inconvenicence or delay. And in thousands of subsequent travel miles together, in several different countries, he never again forgot his passport.

Living behind a famous face which is frequently seen on television, record sleeves and in the press, isn't always easy. Being recognised everywhere is an occupational hazard. Thoroughly exhausted after one television series, he came to have a few days rest with us in Switzerland. High in a picturesque mountain village seemed a safe place for him to walk unrecognised. We wandered into a pharmacy to buy some coffee sweeteners. When leaving, another customer came in. As the door was closing we heard the newcomer ask the lady behind the counter: 'Wasn't that Cliff Richard?'

More remote still, after a cable-car ride to the top of a snow-covered mountain, a waitress in the small cafeteria there requested an autograph.

In London, where the potential of being recognised is greatest, he often seems to 'get away with it' more. I've walked down busy shopping streets with him when no one seemed to catch on. But I've discovered he's developed an immunity to being stared at but not spoken to. Driving down Kensington High Street, he stopped his car at a pedestrian crossing.

'Look,' he said excitedly, 'there's Bryan Forbes, the famous producer!'

At that precise moment, the famous Mr Forbes was doing a good job of crossing the street incognito, whereas about twenty people on the pavement had stopped in their tracks to stare at the young man who was driving me in his silver Jensen.

Shortly after, while stopped at traffic lights, a taxi pulled alongside us. Its female passenger seemed to be suffering an apoplexy. She was jumping up and down, banging the window, waving and blowing kisses in our direction.

Cliff smiled cheerily as he waved to her, muttering to me: 'Can't think who *she* is, but she seems to know *me*!'

Not being recognised can be more embarrassing sometimes. Standing in a milling crowd at Manchester Airport, we were relieved that everyone seemed too preoccupied to notice him or Cindy Kent of 'The Settlers' standing with us.

Then the inevitable happened in the form of two small boys who rushed up with autograph books. They thrust them at Cindy. Cliff smiled approvingly at their 'ladies first' approach and I handed him a pen as Cindy signed. Then, as he stood there with pen poised, the youngsters thanked her politely, retrieved their autograph books and disappeared in the crowd!

'My ego is dented!' joked the unrecognised Mr Richard.

But Cindy could have flown wherever we were going without a plane!

Cliff's professional adviser when travelling is a man I've come to know and appreciate, David Maxwell Bryce. He is not quite as tall as Cliff, carries a little more weight and much less hair. He is by no means old, but has prematurely reached a point of having a beach where the waves used to be! Two more physically dissimilar people, it would be hard to find.

One day, in the North of England, Cliff and David left their hotel for a 'breather'. Walking as 'incognito' as possible around the block, they passed two old ladies who promptly turned and stared at them.

'That's Cliff Richard!' announced one with all the authority of an ageing 'Top of the Pops' fan.

'Oh?' said the other impressed, glancing from David to Cliff and back again, 'Which one?'

David is a true travelling man. He loves planes. In fact, if there's the slightest chance of taking a look at the controls, there's no stopping him. With current skyjack threats, doors to cockpits are usually firmly closed, often locked. And probably there are regulations to dissuade eager passengers from helping to fly planes. But David's healthy interest is quite harmless.

Recognising this on one of our flights, the captain and co-pilot of a large jet welcomed him into the cockpit. Cliff and I were sitting in our seats at the front of the passenger cabin, periodically glancing along the aisle to the cockpit where David was silhouetted in the doorway. Nearing our destination, the seat belt sign came on and, as we strapped ourselves in, we expected David to return at any moment. But no, on this occasion he had hit the jackpot . . . or rather found an accommodating pilot who actually invited him to remain and observe the entire landing procedure. With Cliff and many other passengers I noticed that a little jump seat had been pulled out for David to sit between the men at the controls. The door to the cockpit remained open.

The huge jet turned into its final approach and gracefully descended to the runway. A slight bump on touchdown, the roar of engines reversing, slowing down, and then we started to taxi. It had been a near-perfect landing.

Cliff and I leaned out into the aisle and called up to the cockpit: 'Nice landing, David!' Whereupon several other passengers involuntarily stiffened and froze, suddenly convinced that their landing – and their lives – had been in the hands of an interested amateur aviator!

The journey with Cliff which I'd rather forget began at Jerusalem's Jaffa Gate, continued at breakneck speed through darkened suburbs and ended at a Hungarian Restaurant in Ein Kerem. To be quite accurate, Cliff was in a beat-up van with a couple of strange Arabs and I was in a pursuing four-seater car containing six people.

Seven of us had decided to meet at the Jaffa entrance to the Old City and drive to this Hungarian restaurant which Cliff swore was the best eating place of its kind that side of Budapest. The problem came when I arrived with a tiny four-seater self-drive hire car (it was the only one I could get) and tried to pack seven people inside.

The sight of this was attracting some attention from casual bystanders, and a couple of Arab young men obviously recognised Cliff.

'Don't worry,' said Cliff, when what we were trying to do seemed impossible, 'some of us can get a taxi.'

At this, the two Arabs leapt forward and volunteered: 'Don't get a taxi. We'll take you.'

'Oh thanks,' said Cliff gratefully and, to my surprise, jumped nimbly into their little van.

'What's he doing?' I asked desparingly.

'They'll kidnap him!' suggested one of the others, sensing my concern.

There was no time for more. The little van with its pop star cargo was already disappearing down the road.

'Let's go!' I yelled, and somehow too many people piled into too little car in two seconds flat.

Fortunately the Arabs weren't driving a powerful vehicle, because neither was I. They had the advantage of knowing where they were going, and they got every ounce of power out of their limited engine. I was driving with the disadvantage of having four full-grown men aboard, and my wife almost sitting on my lap!

Dark imaginations made it imperative that I didn't 'lose' the back lights of the van. David would never have let something like this happen, I thought. Large headlines loomed in my imagination: POP STAR PAWN IN ARAB-ISRAEL STRUGGLE. In my mind's eye I caught a brief glimpse of Cliff's mother weeping, and then the scene dissolved to his manager's office in London . . . ' But Dave,' Peter was saying for the umpteenth time, 'I can't imagine you just sitting there and watching him go off with a couple of Arabs!'

A man from Interpol walks in and says: 'We still can't locate where they're holding him.'

An Israeli Embassy official looks up from staring gloomily at the carpet: 'What about our offer of General Dayan as an alternative hostage?'

'Nothing doing, they won't swap him for anyone except the Prime Minister.'

David, pacing the floor in deep thought, suddenly looks up with interest and asks: 'Do you think Mrs Meir would be willing?'

Suddenly I am jerked back to the reality of the present situation by the brake lights of the van ahead.

'He's stopping,' said one of my crammed and by now cramped passengers.

We pulled up behind the little van just as Cliff was

leaping out and waving a cheery goodbye to his new-found Arab friends.

'That was very nice of them,' he commented as he came to where we were erupting out of our small car.

'Here's the restaurant,' he added, and led the way inside.

I breathed a sigh of relief and followed in silence. Golda Meir didn't know what a narrow escape she'd just had!

My most unusual trip with Cliff was sharing a double ski-pull up a Swiss mountain. On his first holiday in Switzerland he took to skis almost like a duck to water. Each day he was out with my 'veteran' skier son, Paul, who, in the circumstances, gave reasonable instruction. My own skiing ability is so lacking that by the end of the week, Cliff was more adept at it than I am.

Stung into action I decided to stop sitting around drinking hot chocolate and join them on a not-too-difficult slope. After livening up the proceedings with a series of spectacular falls, during which novice Richard had remained maddeningly vertical, I reached the ski-pull which would take us to the top again.

Being a double-pull we were able to travel together, side by side. All went well until we reached the end where a very short, sharp track curved down behind a restaurant at the top of the main *piste*. This curve passed the kitchen door beside which the snow was disfigured with various kinds of trash and a thick film of black ash from the boilers.

Seeing Cliff ski past this pollution quite easily, I made a mental note to do no less. That curve must be negotiated at all costs. But my good intentions were not matched by my capabilities. Not only did I fail to make the curve, but I wound up wedged fairly and squarely in the middle of the black ashes!

Being easily recognised isn't always fun. Cliff was having problems at one point in his initial skiing. It was the kind of situation where most people would prefer to suffer the embarrassment of being a rank amateur alone. But at this point two small children, obviously very competent skiers, came gliding down beside us and made a perfect stop right in front of the struggling Cliff. They were less interested in his predicament than in his identity.

'Are you Cliff Richard?' asked one brightly.

'Yes,' admitted Cliff reluctantly, and then added ruefully, 'but right now I wish I wasn't!'

Whenever we have more than brief times together, we are usually working. Often this is in Gospel Concerts which have been arranged all over Europe. The general pattern is to fly in the morning, have a Press Conference on arrival, maybe a radio broadcast or TV appearance, get set up for the evening concert, grab a sandwich . . . and then perform. There are often two performances to two separate audiences the same evening, after which there may well be some kind of reception or certainly the first full meal of the day. Bed is rarely reached until the early hours, and the morning begins with a dawn call to prepare for the flight to the next place where the whole procedure is repeated.

Cliff does such work without pay. Proceeds are given to pre-determined charitable causes. But undoubtedly the greatest bonus from such demanding tours is in the results which follow. These are best indicated in a letter following a Gospel Concert in Sweden. It was not sent to us but to Sweden's leading pop magazine where it was published. The letter was signed simply, 'A girl in the audience'.

'A warm and hearty thanks to Cliff Richard for the Gospel Concert in the Royal Tennishall, Stockholm. Not just because he has a wonderful voice but because he has shown what a fine person he is deep down.

'Much is said about Cliff's conversion and interest in religion as being just a publicity stunt but I, and many others who heard him sing and listened to what he said, can certainly deny that charge. One could feel how he gave himself in his songs, how strongly he felt for that which he sang, and how eagerly he wanted to share it with others.

'Sometimes I felt as if I was sitting in church. I forgot that here before me, in real life, stood my idol of nine years. Instead, here was a young man who very simply, and completely relaxed, could sing with real joy of how happy he was to belong to God. In the song "What A Friend We Have in Jesus", I am certain he wanted to speak to each of us personally.

'I doubt that any artist at any time has won such respect and admiration as Cliff did that evening. I went with a heavy heart because a dear friend had died recently. Actually I wasn't at all inclined to go that night. But when I left I felt joyous and happy because you, Cliff, reminded me of eternal life, of God, of the prayers and Bible-reading we so often neglect but need so desperately.

'Thanks for that evening, Cliff. I shall never forget it.'

Chapter Eighteen

STRANGE CUSTOMS

Going through Customs is not the traumatic experience that infrequent travellers seem to anticipate. With the increase of international travel, most countries are streamlining such formalities, particularly in airports. In Geneva, the arriving air traveller clears Customs *before* he picks up his baggage. If he says he has nothing to declare, the trusting Swiss accept his word; if he does have something he simply gets his case from the conveyor belt and takes it back to a special Customs counter. Similar confidence in the integrity of the traveller is now shown at London Airport where the increasingly popular two-channel system has been adopted. Here the arriving passenger walks through the red channel if he has some thing to declare, and the green channel if he has nothing. It's true that the green channel is subject to spot-checks which may involve a couple of passengers out of every fifty, but the Law of Averages is against you being one of them. That's why it was strange that the first three times I walked through the green channel, over a period of about six weeks, I was spot-checked each time. Being singled out for a spot-check can be embarrassing because other self-righteous passengers tend to pass on the other side convinced that Customs officials have inside information that the poor unfortunate person they've detained is carrying heroin. Firmly convinced that the Law of Averages had gone beserk, I determined not to be spot-checked the fourth time. So I walked through the red channel.

'Yes sir, what do you have to declare?' asked the officer brightly.

'Nothing,' I replied, in a way which he obviously felt was disconcerting.

He looked at me with a 'why-can't-you-read-the-notices-and-understand-the-new-system' look of exasperation.

'If you have nothing to declare,' he said slowly and deliberately, 'you can walk straight through the green lane.'

I looked him straight in the eye and said: 'I chose to come this way and declare nothing rather than going through that green lane to chance the embarrassment of a spot-check for the fourth time in succession!'

He smiled. Most Customs officials are human.

But some have more than tariffs in mind when they examine baggage. In certain countries, political and even religious considerations influence their responsibilities. Before Spain came to terms with its Protestant minority, granting the right of worship and witness, anyone known to be entering the country for the purpose of evangelism (officially known as 'proselytism') could anticipate problems at the border. In fact, if his passport or other documents revealed an objectionable religious affiliation he may not even get into the country.

My first visit to Spain was under such circumstances. Two of us were travelling by train, and with us we had the considerable amount of equipment necessary for presenting 'Gospel Chalk Artistry'. This excellent way of attracting otherwise disinterested people to hear the Christian message entails drawing a large, full-colour Bible picture in full view of an audience, and then displaying it under special lighting effects, including ultraviolet ray. One result of this unusual display is to capture undivided attention of a crowd and earn the right to follow the chalking with talking. The crunch is in the large amount of heavy equipment (stand, board, frame, lights, rheostats, switchboard, chalks, etc.) one has to transport in six separate and somewhat bulky pieces of baggage. If anything is calculated to arouse the interest (and suspicions) of a Customs officer sick of interminably fumbling through other people's dirty underwear, this is it. The fact that in such circumstances I am minimally explicit in describing the function of the stuff adds to the intrigue.

'What is all this?' asked the Spanish official when we were obliged with every other passenger on the train to get off at the frontier station, go through Customs with all our baggage, and then resume our train seats and journey.

'Artist's equipment,' I replied.

'What for?'

'Drawing pictures.'

'Why do you want to do this in Spain?'

'Why not?'

He was beginning to get exasperated, and this was in my pre-Carnegie days before I had read 'How To Win Friends And Influence People'. Finally he showed signs of obvious suspicion and then, with a wicked gleam in his eye, asked: 'Would I be right in thinking that all of these different things work in conjunction with each other?'

I scanned the six equipment packages (he showed not the slightest interest in our personal bags which could have been chock full of diamonds or drugs) and shrugged: 'Yes, that's right.' But the moment I said it, I realised that there was just one dispensable and separate item – a tape recorder, used to provide music synchronised to the picture being drawn.

My positive answer gave him the lead he needed: 'I am afraid I will need to confiscate *one* of these items, but you can reclaim it when you leave the country.'

His strategy was clever . . . and fiendish! Rather than sinking our ship by allowing none of it to enter the country, he preferred to make it even more frustrating by letting us take most of the equipment while rendering it completely useless by his retention of one vital piece. At this point I dearly wanted to make him a present of the tape recorder; the loss of anything else would be catastrophic. But he wasn't going to let us choose what we would leave. His beady eyes scanned the six packages, and then he pointed to one.

'What's in there?' he asked.

'A tape recorder,' I replied trying to suppress my eagerness for him to take it. Then, almost as a way of hiding my true feelings, I pleaded: 'But *please* don't confiscate that. Please . . . *anything* but that. Really, you *must* understand . . . '

The drama was worthy of an Academy Award and, playing before a Spaniard, I piled on the emotion. He appreciated it no end, and the more I pleaded for the tape recorder to be spared the more adamant he was that this should be his 'prize'!

My appearance of anguish as he wrote me a receipt and walked off with the tape recorder almost fooled the friend who was travelling with me. It didn't change until we were safely aboard the train again with every piece of indispensable equipment. The smile of victory we saw on the Spaniard's face as the train pulled out of the station would have changed somewhat if he could have seen two 'crestfallen' characters suddenly go beserk with delight as they disappeared in the direction of Barcelona!

Taking the same equipment across frontiers into Eastern Europe can cause similar problems. When we were planning to cross in to East Germany via Berlin's 'Checkpoint Charlie' we were warned that to get such unusual stuff across one of the most carefully controlled East/West borders would be as miraculous as Moses' little escapade at the Red Sea!

Having crossed that particular border before, I knew the drill. Drive past the American post. Park in front of the East German control point. Go into a building and hand in your passport. Wait anything up to half-an-hour while, somewhere in another room, it is scrutinised and probably photographed. Then, when it is returned, go through to face an official who wants a complete report of all your money in any currency, plus any desirable items such as watch and camera. This is listed on a form to be checked when you return to the West. (The basic idea is to ensure that you do not sell or otherwise dispose of such items on the Black Market in their country.) Then back outside to your car where a long-nosed little man with extremely sharp eyesight asks you to open up everything for the kind of examination that misses nothing. If he's satisfied, you're free to go . . . but it was at this point that my friends in West Berlin foresaw problems. He'll never let that equipment across, they assured me.

On this occasion, my strategy was worked with a knowledge of this procedure. When I was inside the East German border building declaring my watch and noting the number of my camera, I looked up, smiled at the eagle-eyed official assigned to me and in a most friendly and helpful way, volunteered: 'I am an artist, and I am looking forward to painting pictures in your lovely land; in the car outside I have quite a bit of personal equipment for this purpose. Should I note it on this form?'

I could almost see the thought-cloud appear above his peak-cap. In it was a simple artist's easel, a few canvasses, paints, brushes, and so on.

'Yes, yes, you must declare this,' he said eagerly.

I completed the form with the simple notation 'artist's equipment' and looked up with my 'see-what-a-good-boy-am-I' expression. He actually smiled in a satisfied kind of way.

Thus cleared, I walked back out to the car and the ferret-like fellow who was already hovering around it suspiciously. His grin was positively evil! He could see the vehicle was loaded down with things which would brighten his dull day of prodding through contraband-free cars.

'Open it up,' he ordered, pointing to the back.

The first thing he saw was the long wooden box of lighting equipment, and he could hardly wait to look inside. What he saw baffled him because it wasn't immediately identifiable. Normally that's the signal for a grand inquisition, the calling in of 'experts' for advice and many other time-consuming procedures. But I forestalled him.

'By the way,' I said, waving my declaration paper, 'I've cleared all this with the people inside.'

He looked as if I'd just robbed him of his moment of glory. The 'people inside' . . . his superiors . . . they knew about this already? Surely I wasn't trying to pull a fast one if I had readily volunteered information on this weird, unidentifiable equipment to the 'people inside'.

'Yes, look!' I said, taking a calculated risk as I pointed to the words 'artist's equipment' on my declaration list.

Fortunately I was right. While he may have recognised 'watch' or 'camera', his ability to read English did not extend to 'artist's equipment'. The words were meaningless to him, but if they described what I was carrying in the car and if this had been openly declared to the wiser ones inside, who was he to question it? Resigned to the fact that he would have to wait still longer for his moment of glory, he told me to close the back of the car and carry on!

I felt sorry for him, but no pang of conscience for what I'd done. After all, I wasn't taking in dutiable goods to dispose of. My visit was no threat to the seemingly insecure political machine he served. There was not a subversive thought or motive in me. I wasn't planning to shoot Ulbricht or malign Brezhnev; they have their convictions and I have mine. My sole purpose was to meet with fellow members of the Body of Christ and worship Him together. Such a harmless pursuit was really no threat to an inquisitive border guard who had just been the unknowing victim of what has come to be known as 'sanctified smuggling'.

To show how unpredictable our friends on East European borders can be, I was taking the equipment across quite a different border at another time and was forced to explain in detail every bit of my equipment and its contributory function to the final picture. The one thing I omitted to say was the kind of pictures I draw, and where.

'Why are you going to draw pictures in our country?' asked the official.

'You have a very beautiful land,' I said, not really replying to his question.

'What are you going to do with the completed pictures?' he persisted.

'I haven't really thought about it,' I said evasively.

'You must not sell them,' he instructed.

'Oh no, I wouldn't do that,' I said self-righteously, 'if anything I'd give them away.'

'That is also against our laws,' he said.

'All right then,' I suggested, 'I'll bring them all with me when I leave your country.'

'In that case you will need to obtain an export permit first.'

Almost jokingly, I said: 'In that case there is only one other thing to do with my pictures. I'll destroy them!'

'That is a satisfactory solution,' he concluded seriously, and promptly waved me on.

Most European Customs officials speak some English these days. It was not always so. I well remember a hot-tempered Latin type getting mad at me for something I couldn't understand. I stared blankly as he raved and waved, marvelling at his verbosity while he showered me with saliva. Finally the fantastic spate of words subsided with me none the wiser. An eerie silence fell on the scene as, obviously, I was expected to say something. But I couldn't, at least not in his language and, since I had no idea what he was on about, I had nothing to say in English either. The silence was pregnant. He looked at me with a mixture of defiance and expectance. So, slowly and deliberately, I began to recite a soliloquy from 'Macbeth'!

'Is this a dagger that I see before me?' I rasped.

I gained speed and confidence when assured that he didn't understand a bit of it. I started waving my arms and duplicating his histrionics of a few moments before. By the time I was getting to Shakespeare's 'bloody business' bit he was regarding me with the awe and respect of one who has met his match. I thought he was going to applaud by the time I finished, quite exhausted. Instead he smiled and waved me on. I still have no idea what his problem was, but Lord Olivier would have been proud of me!

The tactic most useful in avoiding tiresome questions by Customs officers is diversion. If my man's command of the English language is limited to such phrases as 'Anything to declare?', 'Yes' and 'No', I put on an admiring look and say in surprised tones: 'But you speak *such* good English!' The compliment boosts his ego and, more important, diverts his attention from his main responsibility. He'd feel a rat if he was too hard on such a discerning traveller!

On one such occasion, the officer went on to explain in halting English that he was only just starting to study the language.

'Need any help?' I volunteered.

'Yes,' he said, and pulled his homework book from under the counter.

For the next ten minutes I helped him with some of the intricacies of our language, gained a useful friend in the process, got on first name terms and ensured that when I passed that way again no questions would be asked!

It's not that questions bother me, but just that they can be so tiresome. And sometimes, they lead to interminable red tape with fruitless form-filling. With the exception of Britain and Switzerland, there is rarely any question of paying duty so no dishonesty is involved. It's just that the fewer the questions, the less explanations are needed, the possibility of the intrusion of ridiculous red tape is minimised and precious time is saved. From the Customs officer's viewpoint, he is probably pleased to be relieved of form-filling whenever possible . . . like the two high officials in one European airport.

Diversion, as far as I am concerned, cannot involve lying. Christian convictions do not allow such subterfuge with a clear conscience. So, as on this occasion, when a Customs officer asks me a question which demands a neck-in-the-noose answer, I don't evade the issue. Such was the case here, and out came the inevitable forms (in triplicate). I cannot remember the object in question. Perhaps it was my camera which I had no intention of leaving in his country, but whatever it was he wanted it fully documented with the stamp of approval from higher authority. Resigned to my fate, I settled down to try and remember my grandmother's maiden name and similarly irrelevant questions he was bound to have on his wretched form.

Finally completed, he handed all three copies to me and directed me to the office of the Chief Customs Officer without whose stamp and signature it was not valid. The man in question was important enough to have a secretary who told me he was busy at the moment and I would have to wait. His office door was slightly open and I could hear no sound from within, but she assured me that someone was with him and he must not be disturbed.

I waited for ages with mounting frustration at this time-consuming charade for which I was already scheming ways and means of avoiding the next time I came through here. Finally, when the secretary had to go on an errand, I quietly took courage and tiptoed to the still slightly open door from which no sound came. I peeked in, and there he was at his desk. Sure enough another man *was* with him. Silently, and with the kind of deep concentration which caused them not to notice my presence, they pored over a chess board. No wonder he couldn't be disturbed! They were at a crucial point in the game!

Few pieces were left on the board as I edged into the room. The situation was critical. Two moves and he could be finished. I said nothing. One move was made. He was trapped, and knew it. A look of despair crossed his face as he muttered something I couldn't understand and conceded victory to his opponent.

'That was tough,' I said, sympathetically.

Both men looked up slightly startled.

'Maybe you'll do better next time,' I added, smiling.

'I certainly hope so,' he said, setting up the board for another game.

I jumped in quickly.

'Before you start again, would you mind just signing this?' I asked, thrusting the triplicate form in front of him.

'Certainly,' he said signing without even checking and thumping a rubber stamp on the appropriate part of the form.

'Thanks,' I said gratefully, and left them preparing to do battle once again.

There are some things about Customs officers I'll never understand!

I am often asked which are the easiest Customs through which to go, and which are the most difficult. That's impossible to answer because one cannot generalise. Usually it depends on the particular Customs officer one gets, and which side of the bed he got out that morning. An absolute rule is to avoid women Customs officers at all costs. Without exception, they are worse than men. I've always been thankful not to be an unsuspecting smuggler passing through Warsaw airport because its Customs section is staffed entirely with women.

My toughest experience with Customs was at Dover. I was breezing through Customs with a minimum of personal baggage when a bright young officer in a crisp new uniform asked me to step inside a private office. There he went through my hand-baggage checking everything minutely and searching hard for secret hiding places. Then he asked me to empty my pockets, and went through every single thing in my wallet. Finally I was asked to strip, and my clothing got a similar going over. Then, with no word of explanation or apology he said I was free to go.

My easiest experience with Customs was at a remote Spanish border crossing somewhere high in the Pyrenees. The road was completely deserted. I hadn't seen another vehicle for miles when I reached the frontier to enter Spain and obediently responded to a sign saying 'Stop'. I was there for some time, expecting an officer to come from the little concrete Customs post alongside the road. But nothing happened.

Switching off the engine, I got out of the car and went to investigate. The door was open, and inside was a lone Customs officer sprawled in an armchair and sleeping soundly. The depth of his slumber could be gauged by the emptiness of the wine bottle alongside him.

I turned quietly away, tiptoed back to my car and drove on. If I'd been a real, red-blooded smuggler I would have made a careful note of that place for future reference.

Chapter Nineteen

FRONTIER INCIDENTS

One of the wonderful things about European travel is that, in the West at least, it's possible to cross international frontiers almost as easily as crossing the road. Sometimes even the formality of passport inspection is waved aside.

I never take such privileges for granted. It's something to thank God for. Twice this century, major wars have divided the nations of Europe. For long after the last one countries such as Spain insisted on the necessity of visas. But present ease of international travel, including related implications of the Common Market, are great advantages in Christian service.

We live less than a mile from a Franco-Swiss border. British friends, who live on the opposite side, are almost a stone's throw away from us and yet they are in a different country with different laws and different taxes. To reach them we must cross a frontier which is manned twenty-four hours a day. The crossing is easy. If we forget our passports I doubt if we would be refused entry.

One day, my wife was crossing this border from Switzerland to France. Both Swiss and French immigration officials waved her through when they saw her holding a British passport. On her return journey, the French official waved her through, but the Swiss officer stopped her. She handed over the passport for his examination.

'Is this your passport?' he asked curiously.

'But, of course,' answered Susan, surprised.

'Are you sure?' he insisted.

'Yes,' she said, wondering at his unusual behaviour.

'Is this your picture?' asked the man, showing her the passport picture of her young son.

With the family's four passports sitting in the corner of a drawer, it's easy to be in such a hurry as to pick up the wrong one.

Years ago I was travelling by train through the 'corridor' from West Germany to Berlin. During the customary stop at the border town of Helmstedt, passport and Customs officials worked their way through the train. It was one of my first ventures into Communist territory and I felt a little apprehensive.

'Passport!' demanded the East German officer brusquely as he poked his head into my compartment.

I handed it over.

He gave it a more than superficial examination, glancing at me unnervingly in the process.

'Your name is well-known to us!' he announced.

I was horrified. What did they know about me? Why was I more than an anonymous traveller to them? What was so sinister about my name?

The man handed back my passport and disappeared. It was only later that I realised he was almost certainly thinking of an American politician who was constantly hitting the headlines at that time . . . John Foster Dulles.

East European countries usually grant visas for a specified period. When making application, it is required that the length of stay is stated. I usually add a couple of days to my actual requirement because while they do not mind the visitor leaving before the visa expires, it is a cardinal sin to stay after.

George Hoffman's visa expired when we still required another twenty-four hours in one East European capital. Getting it extended wouldn't be difficult, we thought, but it was a time-consuming chore. If we didn't do it, however, we'd probably be delayed when they discovered this at the airport the following day and that may make us miss our plane.

'Let's go,' we said, heading for the appropriate office.

It was Saturday afternoon and the extremely impressive uniformed and heavily-braided individual who met us at the reception office shook his head. Nothing could be done until Monday morning.

'But we're leaving tomorrow,' we explained.

He continued to shake his head.

'But how can we come here on Monday if we leave tomorrow,' we asked, 'and, more important, how can we leave tomorrow if we cannot get this visa extended today?'

The apparently insoluble problem looked like keeping us there a day longer than we planned when suddenly a slovenly-looking character sidled in. He was quite young and sloppily dressed in a dirty-looking anorak. He hadn't shaved that morning, and a discoloured and obviously home-made cigarette drooped from his lips. He was a sharp contrast to the smartly-uniformed and ramrod stiff Mr Gold Braid.

'What's the problem?' he asked, as if it was something to do with him.

We deigned to explain it to him only because his pretty good command of English might help us to convey the impossible situation to the man who was still insisting on Monday.

'O.K.,' said the newcomer when we finished, 'gimme the passport.'

George handed it over and the man promptly disappeared through a back door.

'I'm stupid!' exclaimed George in a moment of rare candour. 'That fellow's probably a con man who's just stolen my passport!'

He had a point. British passports are valuable documents. Some East Europeans would pay a high price for one. And here were we handing George's to someone who looked like the Communist version of an East End barrow boy!

'George, we're in trouble,' I said, seeing the cold snow of Siberia already reflected in his worried stare. 'Being here with an expired visa is a sin which can be rectified, but being here without a passport is probably punishable by death or dismemberment!'

George didn't think I was funny, and Mr Gold Braid was still standing there poker-faced and uncomprehending.

'Here you are!'

We swung around. It was the slovenly one . . . back . . . with George's passport. And, wonder of wonders, inside was stamped the visa extention.

We looked at the sartorial elegance of old Gold Braid who had been totally unable to help us, and then at the 'tramp' who was the real representative of authority. It taught us something about Communism, but we still can't be quite sure what!

Talking of false impressions, I am reminded of an experience at Passport Control in Amsterdam Airport. The fellow in line ahead of me was the text-book hippie. He looked every inch the part. Handing a grubby American passport to the smartly-uniformed officer, he obviously expected it back after a superficial examination. But he hadn't taken into account the fact that he was arriving in the Dutch capital during a 'Holland hates hippies' period.

Stolid Dutch citizens were getting sick of the flotsam and jetsam of world hippiedom awash in Amsterdam's Dam Square, or sleeping in their lovely parks, or stranded penniless outside the American Express office trying to cadge a lift to anywhere. The answer was obvious. Clamp down on them coming in, especially if they could show no visible means of support.

The fellow before me was a clear candidate for the order of the boot . . . or clog! I listened to the subsequent conversation with interest. The official led off. . . .

'Why are you coming to Holland?'
'Just visiting.'
'How long do you plan to stay?'
'Don't know.'
'Where will you stay in Holland?'
'Haven't decided yet.'
'Where do you plan to go from Holland?'
'I have no idea.'
The atmosphere was getting a little strained.
'How much money do you have?'
The hippie looked insulted.
'Enough,' he said.
'How much do you consider to be enough?' insisted the official, warming to his task and ready for the 'kill'.
'I don't know . . . maybe five thousand dollars!'
The official did a double-take. I nearly dropped my hand-baggage. There were whistles of surprise and murmurs of disbelief all the way back the line of people behind us.
'Let me see it,' said the official, playing his trump card.
The hippie displayed all the dignity he could muster. Then, reaching into his tattered rucksack, produced four fat books of travellers' cheques. The surprised passport official glanced through them quickly. He didn't bother to count. Even I could see there was at least five thousand dollars' worth.

As he waved the fellow through, I was grateful I didn't get the same grilling. Had he pressed me for an answer. I would have had to admit I'd be incapable of paying my one night hotel bill if they wouldn't accept my credit card. But I wasn't questioned. After all, I *looked* respectable!

Few passport officials seem to use their rubber stamps much these days, unless it's a country which needs a visa. Portugal is the lingering exception where they still insist on always marking my passport with a dated entry stamp on arrival and a similar one to record my departure.

One day I was rushing through Lisbon Airport to catch a plane out of the country. I was late checking in and was just about running when I reached Passport Control. Breathless, I handed my passport to the maddeningly slow and precise uniformed official. He thumbed through the pages looking for the entry stamp so that he could put the exit stamp in the customary position alongside it.

Time seemed to drag as he found one or two other Portuguese stamps from previous trips. But these had exit stamps already. Somehow he seemed totally incapable of finding the one page on which a single entry stamp was waiting for his exit stamp to complete yet another pair . . . and meanwhile I had visions of missing my plane.

'Sir,' I pleaded, 'can't you just stamp it anywhere?'

He looked up sharply as if I had uttered some blasphemy! His dark Latin eyes flashed. Suppressed fury was ready to erupt at any minute.

'I veel *not* stamp your passport *anywhere*! I *refuse* to let you leave zee country,' he exclaimed, 'until I prove you arrived!'

Chapter Twenty

A THOUSAND BEDS IN THREE YEARS

An itinerant evangelist friend once threatened to write a book entitled: 'A Thousand Beds in Three Years'. He never did, but I borrow his title to describe my early days of one-night-stands around Britain. I remember six-week stretches of travelling the length of the country sleeping in different beds each night. Brief rest periods back at my Eastbourne home base provided the luxury of the same bed for a few successive nights in one or other of the town's Christian hostelries.

Marriage later led to setting up a home with a bed of my own, but I must admit that, as far as beds are concerned, I never become so attached to the familiar that I find it difficult to get a good night's rest elsewhere. Insomnia is rarely a problem, in fact I have a reputation for being able to sleep anywhere, through anything.

During the 'World Congress on Evangelism' in Berlin, those in charge of room assignments were wondering where to place a notorious snorer. Double occupancy hotel rooms were reserved so someone had to share with him, but those who knew him (some having had first-hand experience of his snoring) were reluctant to volunteer. The man in charge knew it would be asking for trouble to wriggle out of this by assigning some poor unsuspecting individual not acquainted with the problem.

When I heard about it, I volunteered to share immediately. This was no act of bravado. The chronic snorer was a personal friend with whom I had roomed before, and in whose home I had stayed. I had heard him snore and, even though a revving motorcycle would have had difficulty competing, I knew it wouldn't disturb me. Sure enough, on the first night of sharing, I slept soundly. But later the next day I was surprised to see a concerned-looking Congress official who said he was trying to solve a problem about snoring in a certain room. When he mentioned our room number, I told him to relax, that there must be some mistake because I was the person sharing that room and I had registered no complaint.

'I know that,' he told me, 'but it's the occupant of the *next* room who can't sleep!'

The increasing popularity of central heating in Britain decreases problems once faced by visiting American evangelists who had never slept in unheated bedrooms. One of those who toured post-war Britain before its present level of affluence, returned to the United States to be questioned by curious fellow-countrymen.

'Is it true they have no refrigerators in British homes?' was a frequent question, to which he replied: 'No, that's quite untrue; in fact, every British home I was in had at least *two* refrigerators . . . only *they* call them bedrooms!'

Another transatlantic type was staying at a terraced house in South Wales. After the entire household retired for the night, he shivered under what for him were totally inadequate bedcovers. He put on a couple of sweaters, laid his heavy overcoat across the bed and tried to settle again. Still he shivered. Looking around the room, he had an idea. Curtains could be easily unhooked and replaced before he vacated the room for breakfast in the morning. No one need know, he thought, as he laid them across the bed. But an hour later he was still wrestling with the problem of cold. There was only one other way of adding to his covering, and this was by utilising strips of floor carpeting. It did the trick. Once he laid the carpeting over his bed, he soon fell fast asleep.

But his plan to replace everything as he found it before he descended at a pre-arranged time for breakfast came adrift. He hadn't counted on that delightful facet of British hospitality where the host creeps in at the crack of dawn to awake the guest with a nice cup of tea!

The Welsh must also capture credit for getting the fullest possible use out of a bed. In normal circumstances this item of furniture is used an average of eight hours in twenty-four, but not so where a fellow-evangelist once found himself. There he was asked if he would mind getting up by a certain time in the morning, and was also warned that he would not be able to use the room during the day or retire before a particular hour each night. It seemed that the father and son of the house worked different shifts in the mines. Both used the same bed at different times of the day, in fact, once my friend was fitted into the bed schedule it was in constant use twenty-four hours a day!

One of the worst beds I ever experienced was in southern Europe. The hotel was rated third class, but it could claim running water in the rooms. In mine, it ran down the walls. Unfortunately it was absorbed by the sodden and disintegrating plaster before reaching floor level, otherwise it may have served a useful purpose in drowning several cockroaches which scuttled away each time I switched on the light! The bed, set in the middle of a bare, dirt-encrusted floor, had to be seen to be believed. Its lumpy straw mattress was decidedly damp so I got the idea of tossing it aside and sleeping on the springs, only to find that these had long since collapsed and were replaced by boards nailed across the frame.

The situation reminded me of a cartoon in which a monk was being shown some bare wooden beds of the kind on which they are reputed to sleep. The salesman was asking: 'Would you prefer hard wood or soft wood, sir?'

Eastern Europe presents an interesting situation where,

in many cases, homes have no bedrooms. Apartments are often so small that it is impossible to indulge in the luxury of having even one room used exclusively for sleeping. Thus I have stayed in many homes where lounge, dining room and even kitchen are regularly transformed into sleeping quarters at the appropriate time. In such situations it is often taken for granted that the guest sleeps with the host or that everyone beds down in different parts of the same room. One room in which I slept many times has accommodated up to fourteen people.

On one occasion in Yugoslavia, four male members of a team I was leading were told they would be sleeping in a newly-constructed house. What we didn't know until we got there late at night was that the place was still not finished, and our room was about the only one anywhere near habitable. It was furnished with one wide and incredibly long double bed. The problem of how to fit four of us into it was solved by three of the group laying side-by-side the traditional way, while the fourth fellow lay at a ninety-degree angle to the rest at the bottom of the bed.

Hotel beds range from simple to sophisticated. They vary in cleanliness from those in which sheets are changed every day, to some in more remote areas where it seems the same bed linen is used by a succession of guests.

Attachments to beds become ever more intriguing. For instance, there are those with built-in massage apparatus. Drop a coin in a bedside box and the bed comes to life, vibrating continuously for about fifteen minutes. Strangely enough, I have found these so relaxing that never yet have I been aware of the thing switching off. By that time, I am always asleep.

Headboards were once simple attachments at the top of a hotel bed . . . plain and functional. Then someone had the idea of installing a light switch in them, later to be followed by a small built-in reading lamp. Radio speakers came next, with the appropriate buttons to operate them. A further series of buttons serves to operate all lights, including those in the bathroom, for the benefit of forgetful types who are also too lazy to get out of bed again. Thermostatic controls for central heating came next. In one headboard I found all the buttons and knobs necessary for remote-controlling a television set in the far corner of the room. In fact, these attachments to beds are now becoming so complicated that the porter taking the guest to his room is likely to need a degree in electronics to be able to explain the uses of all this paraphernalia!

I know one airline pilot who breezes his way through using the incredibly complicated mass of levers, buttons and dials in the average jet-age cockpit, but is quite incapable of coping with modern hotel headboards in some places where he has night stops.

Bedrooms that bother me most are those in Eastern Europe which are bugged with listening devices. This is commonplace in Communist countries so that I make a point never to discuss private matters in hotel rooms. When sharing a room with a colleague on one occasion, he switched off the light and said: 'Goodnight Dave'. Then, as an afterthought, he added: 'And to all our listeners, this is the end of broadcasting for today!'

To avoid the possibility of an innocuous hotel room conversation being misinterpreted by whoever is listening or taping it, separate rooms for single occupancy are usually used. Since I am not in the habit of consciously talking to myself, this means there is nothing much for the eavesdropper to hear. But, according to my wife, I sometimes talk in my sleep. She assures me that these utterances are so incomprehensible that they cannot even be recognised as English. This has often caused me to conjure up pictures of Secret Policemen in Eastern Europe, frustration written all over their faces, listening to a tape they cannot understand. My vision even extends to linguistic experts being called in to solve the problem of what the guest in Room 303 of the People's Hotel was preaching with such ferocity at three in the morning!

Sometimes I am forced to use substitute beds such as a bench in an airport or the seat of my car. Fortunately the latter has completely reclinable front seats so this is no chore if I can manage to keep warm. One night I was driving south on the German autobahn between Frankfurt and Basle when I ran into the most amazing snowstorm I ever experienced. It was so hard that visibility was reduced to almost nil, and very soon all traffic was grinding to a halt in an ever-increasing depth of snow. Fortunately I was able to make it to the next parking area where I became bogged down in comparative safety. Far from the nearest town, there was little I could do except settle down to sleep until morning. But this raised a problem. The stationary car soon became very cold, while the only way to warm it was to leave the engine running and the heater on. This, in turn, presented the risk of the exhaust pipe getting clogged with snow, deadly fumes being forced back into the car and my sleep becoming too sound for safety. It was a long night of dozing in pleasant warmth, alternated with quick excursions into the raging blizzard to make sure the exhaust pipe was still clear.

Usually I sleep in the car only on all-night drives when a comparatively quick nap in the early hours sets me up to continue safely through until morning. One such night I was driving to a certain British city where an all-night prayer meeting was in progress so I knew that someone would be around at whatever time I arrived. Not many miles from my destination, the desire to sleep caught up with me, so I pulled off into a deserted parking area and slept for about thirty minutes. When I awoke it was about three a.m., and pitch dark. I fumbled with the ignition and started the car. Then I switched on the headlights and thought I was dreaming. In the beams were policemen, armed and menacing! I blinked, shook my head and looked again. They were still there. It was most disconcerting. I glanced sideways and saw more shadowy figures. I was sure they were behind me too. By this time I was fully awake and decided to do the only logical thing; I wound down my window and greeted the nearest representative of the law with a cheery: 'Good morning officer!'

Ignoring my attempt to be friendly, he asked: 'What are you doing here?'

'Until a few moments ago, I was sleeping,' I replied.

'Where do you think you're going now?' he asked.

'To a prayer meeting,' I said quite truthfully, but obviously unconvincingly.

'To a *what*?' he asked.

He took a lot of convincing. My licence was checked. Then the car papers. Finally the tense atmosphere subsided, and the men surrounding me relaxed. I was told they were searching for someone who had committed a murder in the vicinity. I fitted the description of the wanted man.

A similar experience occurred after bringing a minibus across the English Channel by the night car ferry. Arriving at my destination in the South of England, I could not disturb those to whom I was delivering the vehicle until a reasonable hour of the morning. As it was fitted with bunks in the back, I drove it to a quiet part of town, parked in an unrestricted side road and bedded down for the rest of the night.

I wasn't sure how long I slept before I heard a tapping on one of the windows. A torch was being shone in. Bleary-eyed I tried to avoid the beam to see who was behind it. There was a police car.

'What's the matter?' I asked the two officers.

'What are you doing here?'

I explained the situation, which they accepted but were obviously unimpressed.

'You can't sleep here,' they said.

'Am I parked in a restricted area?' I asked.

'No,' they admitted reluctantly.

'Is there any law against sleeping in a parked vehicle?'

'Well, er . . . no,' they said.

'So what's the problem?'

'The local council wouldn't like it,' suggested one.

'But unless we wake them all now, we can't be sure, can we?' I replied.

Recognising defeat, one policeman told me to 'forget it', and both left me to continue sleeping until morning.

One occasion when my inbuilt timing mechanism failed me was at a parking area just off the Italian Autostrada near Turin. It was the night of a special meeting addressed by Billy Graham. I had been invited to stay in the Turin hotel where he and his associates were spending the night before leaving for Venice the following day. Since our ultimate destination was Zagreb, Yugoslavia, I declined the offer by saying that I wanted to move on that night to cover more miles with less traffic. Having started, however, I began to feel very tired . . . possibly because I had driven from Geneva, Switzerland, earlier that day. I pulled off into a parking area at about midnight, deciding on a quick nap for half-an-hour. The night was warm and the reclinable car seat was comfortable. I slept well. Too well.

When I awoke the sun was shining and heavy traffic rumbled along the Autostrada. I glanced at my watch. Seven-thirty! I couldn't believe it, but the stiffness of my joints endorsed the fact that I had slept soundly all night. I got out and walked around the car . . . yawned . . . stretched . . . and then saw a familiar car sweep by. It was the one carrying Mr Graham.

I jumped back into my own car and started out on to the Autostrada. Soon I overtook the Graham car and signalled to Dr Robert Evans who was driving. We pulled in at the next filling station, at which point I realised the embarrassing situation I would need to explain. I had not driven throughout the night, but had slept in a car when a comfortable hotel room had been offered me.

'Where did you sleep?' they asked me.

I grinned, and replied: 'Oh, I found a nice little place just outside town.'

They were too polite to ask me why my 'nice little place' failed to provide facilities for me to shave!

Chapter Twenty-One

VARIED MENU

Someone claimed that when God calls us to walk a stony pathway, He provides strong shoes. To which I would add that when God directs a person to an international itinerant ministry, He strengthens his stomach too.

Perhaps the travelling Christian worker should re-write the old hymn of dedication –

Where He leads me, I will follow;
What He feeds me, I will swallow.

Sometimes I am in situations where I pray for a dulling of the sensitivity of my tastebuds, strengthening of my stomach and 'special enabling' for my digestive system.

But I must admit that being British is a disadvantage because of our in-built suspicion of culinary innovation. Having lived on the Continent for nearly ten years, I can understand European views of British eating habits. They tend to feel we suffer a sort of meal-time myopia which prevents us seeing more than meat and two veg, or fish and chips, as satisfactory sustenance. That's why the first Costa Brava restauranteur to put up a sign advertis-ing 'fish and chips' could hardly cope with the British tourist customers. Now everyone's in on the act and signs such as 'a good cup of tea – just like home' abound. In fact the Costa Brava in summer has got to be just an annexe of Brighton or Blackpool.

Continual travel to and fro across the Continent has broadened my feeding horizons immeasurably. When I eat in the restaurant of the Park Hotel, Prague, and I see 'Strawberry Soup' among the Starters, I know it's not a misprint but a delightful prelude to the main course which, in Czechoslovakia, is likely to include that relic of my Westcountry childhood, dumplings. (Why the people of Plymouth and Prague share a bias toward these mushy, gravy-covered splodges I'll never know!) Down in the Alsace region of France, I was served cow's udder which may sound revolting to many, but is really quite acceptable. Snails and frogs' legs aren't bad either. Octopus I avoid only because I am not keen on any seafoods. I do draw a definite line when it comes to chocolate-covered ants. (Those addicted insect-eaters who try to persuade me otherwise assure me that these are 'just like chocolate-covered currants', which endorses my desire to settle for the currants).

Some nationalities do strange things with perfectly recognisable and acceptable food. The Dutch eat bacon raw, and spread jam on cheese. (I've learned to like only the latter). Europeans look askance at Americans who spread marmalade on fried bacon, put mayonnaise on tinned (sorry 'canned') peaches, drink coffee with their main course and iced water with everything! Likewise, my American friends cringe when served with a bottle of unrefrigerated Coca Cola – without ice. And they cannot understand why Europeans consider 'corn-on-the-cob' and pumpkin unfit for human consumption. (The latter features in one of America's meals of the year as a dessert pie. But when we tried to buy a pumpkin from a Yugoslav farmer for this purpose, he was horrified and refused to accept payment so that he would enjoy no monetary gain from our 'misguided' ideas. As we walked off with our huge pumpkin, he was still shaking his head in disbelief while continuing to chop up others for his cattle).

The first time my wife and I were invited to a Swiss home for an evening meal, I was warned that the hospitality was liable to be lavish so I didn't eat all day. By evening I was ravenous.

'I could eat a horse!' I told my wife as we were about to ring the bell.

'Good,' she replied, 'that's the main course tonight.'

The Swiss hostess had contacted Susan and asked if we would mind eating pony meat – a real delicacy. My wife, putting aside any thoughts of World War II austerity eating, said she was sure it would be delightful. And it was.

Scandinavians like reindeer meat, and so do I. A surprising number of my Scots friends turn up their noses at haggis, and so do I.

It's strange, but true, that the worst *pizza* I ever tasted (and I love the stuff) was in Italy. The poorest *Wiener Schnitzel* (usually a sure-fire winner anywhere) was in Vienna. And the most revolting *goulash* was served me in Hungary. I have never visited China and am reluctant to do so because, at the moment, I enjoy Chinese food.

Maybe it's my love of fresh fruit and vegetables which makes me starry-eyed at the thought of eating in Israel. Usually I eat very light breakfasts, but the habit is broken the moment I step inside an Israeli kibbutz. They serve the most amazing breakfast meals which include fresh cucumber, radishes and celery. They can stir up my Zionist tendencies just by serving me breakfast! But Israel must also be recorded as the place where I was served the most revolting coffee I ever tasted – by an otherwise friendly and hospitable Bedouin at his encampment in the middle of the Negev Desert. Although I am strongly against avoidable pollution, I must confess to surreptitiously staining the desert with all but the first sip of this revolting brew.

A similar experience led to the one occasion when my stomach gave up in disgust and I wound up in the only hospital bed I ever occupied. I can remember coming slowly to the surface of subconscious delirium to hear the doctor in a Karachi hospital affirming to the staff nurse that it was 'the worst case of dysentry' he had seen.

Later, prior to my release, he came by and asked me where I'd been eating before becoming ill. The places I mentioned were acceptable, and he was puzzled as to where I picked up the germ.

'I did drink a cup of tea with some frontier guards out on the desert,' I added.

He grinned, his problem solved.

'Go visit them again,' he said, 'see how they make it – but don't drink any more of it.'

A few days later, I was out on the blazing desert with my friends at the guard encampment. I explained I had been in hospital, so would not eat or drink today.

'But, as a matter of interest,' I asked them, 'how do you manage to make tea in this remote area?'

They explained that their periods of duty lasted a couple of weeks. At the beginning of this time, they filled a huge cauldron with water, heated it over a fire and emptied into it their entire ration of loose tea. Ever after this, the cauldron was simply reheated whenever they wanted tea. The full cauldron lasted them the entire two weeks.

Quite apart from the staleness of the tea after constant cooling and reheating, tiny insects (and occasionally larger livestock) would crawl up the side of the cauldron and fall in. The ones that didn't drown were boiled alive the next time around. In any event, no one was served tea with *live* insects in it, but the leaves at the bottom of the cup could justifiably be examined with suspicion.

A comparatively recent incident proves that even the finest eating places can present problems. In a certain West European capital, a friend invited Cliff Richard, Bill Latham and me to join him for lunch in the lavish surroundings of an American-owned luxury hotel. For Cliff it was a pleasant change from BBC canteen sandwiches, and for Bill and me the rare privilege of being able to look at the left side of the menu without casting anxious glances to the right. We were grateful for the generosity of our host.

Walking into the restaurant, I couldn't help noticing the number of sidelong glances in our direction, accompanied by whispers of recognition for Cliff.

The meal was delightful, except for one thing. There was a dead fly in my side salad. I couldn't believe my eyes in such a sumptuous setting, but there it was, as large as life and as dead as a dodo!

No one else had noticed it, but it put me in a predicament. Obviously a complaint should be registered and, if I had been paying the bill I am quite sure I would have got the meal for nothing – if only to keep me quiet. But two things caused me to reconsider. First, we were guests of a gracious host to whom I didn't want to bring embarrassment. Secondly, for Cliff's sake, I didn't want to draw further attention to 'his' table. So I covered the corpse with a lettuce leaf, and left it.

Back at our own hotel, Bill was commenting about how we wouldn't need to eat for days after a meal like that, and I was wondering 'shall I or shan't I?'

Finally, I said: 'Fellows, I hate to dampen any enthusiasm, but frankly I was disgusted that a first-class restaurant would allow a dead fly to find its way into my salad.'

Cliff looked intrigued.

'There was a dead fly in your salad?' he asked, as if to be sure.

'Yes,' I said.

'That's funny,' he said with a bemused expression on his face, 'there was one in mine too!'

Chapter Twenty-Two

O FOR A THOUSAND TONGUES

'How many languages do you speak?'

The frequent question is usually posed with keen anticipation. Those who ask it are convinced that someone who constantly visits so many different language areas must be proficient in a number of tongues. In point of fact, it is the very diversity of the languages in the places to which I travel which makes it virtually impossible to think of achieving any kind of proficiency in them.

The other mark against me is that I do not have a natural aptitude for languages.

French is the language of the area in which we live. Susan has achieved a remarkable fluency in it. For the children, it is spoken with the same ease and lack of foreign accent as their mother tongue. As for me, I speak with such confidence the limited amount I need to survive, that French-speaking listeners get an impression of my linguistic ability which far exceeds my tiny vocabulary.

Alison made a shrewd assessment when she asked: 'Mummy, why is it we speak French and Daddy only says the words?'

Often I've longed for the ability to learn a new language with the ease of a small child. When Paul first went out to play in Switzerland, it was with children who were as completely ignorant of English as he was French. But they seemed to communicate reasonably well. After some weeks we tried to get our small son to share with us some of the French he had learned, but in a home where English was always spoken this pre-schooler saw no point in it.

'Maybe he hasn't learned any,' suggested Susan, since neither of us had heard him utter a word of French.

Then, one day, I arrived home to see him standing outside chatting to a little Swiss boy. He hadn't seen me so I sidled across out of his line of vision but within earshot. I was amazed! There was my own little boy rattling off a foreign language with the fluency of a French radio commentator. I couldn't contain myself.

'Paul,' I yelled enthusiastically, 'you're speaking French marvellously!'

He glanced up, surprised to see me but reflecting not an iota of my obvious joy at his linguistic prowess.

'I have to speak French,' he said, pointing to his small and now rather bewildered friend. 'He doesn't speak English!'

Paul's fluency in French is still functional, never flamboyant.

A child's ease of communication was best demonstrated when he started attending a kindergarten which sounded like the Tower of Babel. Children of many mother tongues happily played together unhampered by language limitations. One day I asked one of Paul's friends how old he was.

'I am *quatre ans*,' he said without batting an eyelid.

Most of my present work is with Christian leaders and others who speak English with varying degrees of fluency. I may know a few key phrases in their language and, when no one's listening, we cope remarkably well. But in public meetings I have always used interpreters. Strangely enough, this is not such a distraction or difficulty as some seem to imagine . . . provided the interpreter is a good one.

Speaking through an interpreter calls for various ground rules. A speaker may as well recognise before he starts on an alliterated outline that the link-up between his cleverly conceived points will be lost in translation. I heard one fellow preaching his first sermon to a foreign congregation choosing as his theme an acrostic on the word LOVE. By the time he was halfway through his sermon, he was wondering how soon he could leave for home and the interpreter was on the point of nervous breakdown!

Colloquial expressions are out. This is illustrated by the old story of the preacher who began: 'I'm tickled to death to be here.' The bewildered interpreter couldn't handle that one so simply explained to his people: 'I cannot quite understand what he means but he seems to be saying that due to his being here he is squeezing himself until he dies!'

One night in Italy, Billy Graham used one of his favourite illustrations about an ant-hill. The sermon was interrupted as the term had to be explained to an otherwise excellent interpreter. A couple of days later I was with Mr Graham in another country. His interpreter was an old friend of mine so I caught him just before he went on to the platform.

'Do you know what an ant-hill is?' I asked him.

'A what?'

I explained and added: 'I don't know what he's preaching about tonight, but he may use that illustration.'

Sure enough, partway through the sermon the evangelist started on his ant-hill story. As he waited for the first phrase to be interpreted, he cast a sidelong and slightly apprehensive glance at his interpreter.

My friend sailed into it as if he had known the term for years rather than just a few minutes!

Humour can be lost when speaking to those of another culture. On one occasion when I was using a sermon illustration about my wife, I commented lightheartedly: 'She's the best wife I ever had!' The godly pastor who was interpreting stopped short with a shocked expression on his face. Hurriedly and in hushed tones he spoke to me in

English: 'I can't interpret that. In our country, Christians have only one wife. It would be unwise to mention you have had more!'

Congregations appreciate it if the visitor can say something in their language, so sometimes I begin with a greeting which needs no interpretation. In one particularly difficult Slavic language, I was trying to learn such an opening sentence phonetically. I practised hard with my interpreter trying to correct my accent and intonations. Finally, when I said it from the pulpit I noticed some people in the front row beginning to weep. Later I told my interpreter: 'They must have appreciated my attempt to say something in their language; did you notice some of the people were moved to tears?'

He had the uncomfortable look of someone reluctant to break bad news.

'Dave,' he said with a note of despair, 'when you spoke from the pulpit you forgot all I told you about accent and intonation. What you said was barely understandable. Those must have been tears of mourning for the way you murdered our language!'

Peter Smith is a singer with whom I've been privileged to work on many occasions. His ability to learn songs phonetically in another language is excellent, but one section of his repertoire is impossible to translate. While universally appreciated, Negro Spirituals must be sung in English to be truly effective. But when Peter sings them in another language area, he feels that to raise the song above the level of mere entertainment it is necessary for him to explain through an interpreter its theme and meaning.

In Portugal one day, he was introducing a well-known Negro Spiritual through a very excellent interpreter, and concluded: 'And so I am going to sing "Swing Low Sweet Chariot" '. The interpreter looked startled. For the life of him he could not think of the Portuguese word for 'chariot'. But he did his best. He used the closest thing he could think of on the spur of the moment and, in Portuguese, it came out 'Swing Low Little Donkey Cart'!

My biggest muddle in the matter of communicating in another language occurred in Spain during a family holiday. Spaniards don't go to bed early at the best of times and, as a 'night bird' myself, it doesn't usually bother me. But when I am on holiday I enjoy indulging in the unaccustomed luxury of early nights. The noise in the tiny street where our little hotel was situated regularly reverberated until well after midnight. While nothing keeps me awake when I want to go to sleep, Susan seems to find it less easy to stay asleep during ear-splitting sounds of riotous living!

She bore it bravely for several nights, but her patience was strained considerably when at one o'clock one morning even the usual sounds of revelry were drowned by the sound of a pick hacking at the road outside. After confirming that two men were in fact engaged in nocturnal road digging, she came in from the balcony and woke me.

'This is the end!' she exclaimed, 'They're actually digging up the road outside!'

I stumbled out of bed on to the balcony. Several other people appeared in night-clothes on other balconies and at windows to view the curious scene below. The two men had succeeded in digging a hole of considerable depth in which one was standing up to his knees in sewage. The other one was directing him to dig further along when suddenly, as if on cue, several of the observers including myself suggested they call it a day . . . or a night!

Various languages were used to impress the point on the guilty couple, and some of the words were ones I hadn't heard before.

The diggers, hardly acknowledging the outburst of protest, continued with what was obviously a self-imposed task. It was clear they were not local council workers on night shift, and I began to wonder whether they had any authorisation for their activity. By now they had demolished a fair bit of pavement.

I pulled on a raincoat over my pyjamas and went downstairs. My Spanish was limited to little more than greeting them, and even '*Buenos dias*' seemed somewhat inappropriate in the small hours of the morning. Spanish illiteracy was more than compensated by international sign-language of which I am a master! I pointed at them accusingly. 'Bang-bang' I yelled, indicating what they were doing. Then I folded my hands to form a pillow, rested my head on them as if trying to sleep. Finally I threw up my hands and said: 'Impossible!' For good measure I pointed up to all the pyjama-clad onlookers who were fast losing interest in the diggers, obviously more impressed by the theatrical quality of my antics.

The diggers understood perfectly, but made it obvious they had no intention of stopping. One snarled something unintelligible and the other raised his pick in my direction. I ducked instinctively. He turned to the hole and continued hacking.

That finished it! Any thoughts of gracious understanding and the preservation of international relationships were dispelled. They could have the Rock of Gibraltar as far as I was concerned, but unless they quit digging at this time of night I was going to complain to the police. Having got this point across to them, I stalked off up the road toward the police station stopping only briefly at the end of the street to see if this impressed them. They were too busy digging to look.

Pushing through shirt-sleeved and summer dressed crowds coming from the many little bars and cafes even at that time of night, I must have looked a curious sight in pyjamas and raincoat, but I made it to the police station. As I marched in, the lone representative of law and order on duty smartly pulled his feet off his desk and pushed a wine bottle under it.

'*Buenos dias*,' I said.

'Eh?' he shook his head as if to clear it, and glanced up

at the station clock to make sure it really was two in the morning.

'Do you *hablo Ingles*?' I asked.

He shook his head.

'Well, listen carefully,' I said, and proceeded to perform my mime of the situation from the last arm-swinging bang-bang to the head on 'pillowed' hands representation of sleep and the final gesture of despair at its impossibility.

A look of abject horror appeared on the bewhiskered face of that Spanish policeman.

'Stop!' he yelled, probably using the only English word he knew, and indicating I should stay right where I was.

He disappeared out the door and down the street. Seconds later he reappeared, breathless, with another similarly gasping Spaniard in waiter's uniform.

'I speaka zee Eengleesh,' said the newcomer urgently, 'I veel translate. Zee police, he ask where it happens.'

I told him the name of the street which they both understood.

'And how many people?'

I assumed they wanted to know the number of people being disturbed, so I said: 'Maybe twenty.'

When this was translated I thought the little policeman was going to expire on the spot. He clapped one hand to his forehead and steadied himself against the wall with the other. A hoarse whisper proceeded from his lips.

The waiter thought for a moment, and then asked: 'Zee police, he say are they all dead?'

At that moment I knew I was encountering a communication problem. My bang-bang to the policeman had indicated a gun. The mime for sleep had been interpreted as death or at least injury. And the thought of some maniac shooting as many as twenty people was just too much for him!

The waiter helped me explain the true situation, and

the relieved policeman said that since he was alone on duty he could not come to investigate but inquiries would be made in the morning.

I gave up. I thanked the waiter and wandered dispiritedly from the police station. The policeman was mopping his brow with one hand and reaching under his desk with the other.

When I returned to the hotel, the men had stopped digging and everyone else had gone to bed. In the morning it was explained to me that a sewage problem had made it imperative for the road to be dug up immediately. The offending hole was still half-filled with smelly water and some planks of wood were ineffectively covering it. Evidently the urgency had disappeared in the cold light of dawn because ten days later, when we left for home, the hole was still disfiguring the roadway. Everyone had become accustomed to it.

Chapter Twenty-Three

THE ETERNAL TRAVELLER

I hurried down the familiar corridors of Amsterdam's Schipol Airport recently, just ahead of the rest of the crowd from my incoming flight. I was first at the Passport Control point which achieved my objective of not having to waste time standing in line.

'Where did you come from?' the uniformed officer enquired as he opened my passport.

The question was quite normal. When any new influx of passengers appears, he needs to know where they came from in case there are any special health regulations or other points peculiar to their point of embarkation. The officer invariably addresses the question to the first passenger of an incoming plane-load.

But on this particular day, my mind went blank. I was just completing a particularly mobile week. I'd been to many places. I was desperately tired. My memory was giving up. He asked a simple question, but *I could not remember where I caught that plane less than two hours before*!

'Copenhagen,' said the person behind me.

'Yes, that's right . . . Copenhagen,' I agreed, giving a good impression of an absent-minded professor.

How could I have forgotten? How stupid! And maybe my slowness seemed suspicious to the officer.

'How long are you staying in Holland?' he asked.

'I'm not sure,' I answered truthfully but, as far as he was concerned, not very satisfactorily. The point was, if I could complete my business fast enough, I might be able to catch an evening plane to Geneva. If not, I would be there overnight.

'Where are you going from here?' was his third and last question.

'Switzerland,' I said confidently and without hesitation. 'I live there.'

He handed back my passport and waved me through with, 'Have a nice stay in Holland.'

The Dutchman's three questions are ones I find people – especially young people – asking everywhere. In a much broader sense, twentieth century man looks around his sick and crumbling world. He sees war, hatred, anarchy, crises. He becomes increasingly concerned about the rising threat of pollution on his planet. He is bothered by the inequity of a civilisation where some of his fellow-beings have huge food surpluses while statisticians report others dying of starvation at the rate of ten thousand per day.

Where did I come from?

How long am I to be here? Why? And what's the point anyway?

Where am I going?

Failure to find answers has opened the door to all kinds of philosophies promoted by a multitude of 'messiahs'. Humanists claim that man must begin with himself and work out his own salvation in a continuing evolutionary process. Prophets of permissiveness are not simply content to propagate violation of accepted moral guidelines, but call for their total eradication. An upsurge of interest in some of the most irrational and lunatic aspects of Eastern religions indicates the desperation of some in searching for answers. And amid the cacophony of 'salvation' promises are those sad, pathetic and spiritually sterile religious philosophers who disguise dead theology in the terms of historic Christianity.

My fellow Swiss-resident and friend Francis Schaeffer

made a shrewd analysis of the current scene when he claimed that young intellectuals 'have no answers for their Universe, and without an answer they can do little more than withdraw from life or else lash out in frustration against it.'

There are answers, and I find that at last the dust is being blown off many long-neglected Bibles to find them. The answers God gives are basic and consistent. They don't change with the times, and yet they are relevant to all eras of history. They are as contemporary as tomorrow's newspaper. Thousands of young people, some who were slaves to drugs and despair, have awakened to this fact and sparked off the comparatively new, spontaneous and now worldwide 'Jesus Revolution'.

Time and again, I am asked how I view the world scene in the course of my travels. Questioners may be hopeful that I have a new and more optimistic slant on things than one who sits at a single vantage point. I have. And what I see first-hand, supplemented by what I know of current events in areas beyond my own travel limits, matches what I read in the Bible.

In country after country I see not just a few but many people who are truly fearful about the future. Few successfully employ the shock absorbers of false security when they *know* that battle-ready nuclear submarines constantly patrol the oceans below us. Land-based nuclear warheads with unthinkable destructive power are poised ready to blow our planet apart. And now plans are already being implemented to make possible the placing of nuclear space stations in orbit with increased ease of striking any spot on earth.

'It'll only take one madman to push the panic button . . . ' is a view I've heard expressed many times in various ways, but usually as an unfinished sentence.

Then I turn to the Bible's description of man's reaction as civilisation approaches a predicted climax: '*The courage of many people will falter because of the fearful fate they see coming upon the earth . . .* ' (Luke 21:26 LB)

I see leaders, national, political and economic, perplexed by the apparently insoluble problems before them. In one royal palace of Europe, I was privileged to be in the private study of the occupant. I was surprised to see on the wall a plaque bearing the question of the Apostle Paul quoted in Acts 9:6, '*Lord, what wilt thou have me to do*?' At least one leader appeared to be looking in the right direction for guidance in the perplexity of his responsibilities.

Again I turn to the Bible prediction that '*the nations will be in turmoil, perplexed*' (Luke 21:25 LB)

I see the trend of devaluing the beautiful gift of sex God gave us, with pornography and perversion taking over. Live sex shows in some countries of Europe. The Playboy philosophy and a subsequent sex obsession in the United States. Easy abortion for those whose sexual 'freedom' backfires. Homosexuality not only condoned, but commended. Venereal disease reaching epidemic proportions.

Then I remember the Bible's record of Jesus prophesying ' . . . *the world will be as indifferent to the things of God as the people were in Noah's day . . . and the world will be as it was in the days of Lot . . .* ' (Luke 17:26,28 LB)

Mrs Billy Graham once said: 'If God doesn't judge the world soon, He will have to apologise to Sodom and Gomorrah!'

I see the enigma of the 'haves' and 'have nots', the 'over-fed and the hungry'. From this I see such innovations as TEAR Fund putting Christian compassion into action, and an increase among evangelicals of social as well as spiritual concern for their fellow-beings. And then I see Jesus predicted the need for such developments when he said: '*There will be famines . . . in many places*' (Matt. 24:7 LB)

I read that 'a professional seismologist has estimated that there has been more than a 2,000 per cent increase in major earthquakes in the mid-twentieth century over the

the mid-fifteenth', and I remember that in the same breath as famines, Jesus pinpointed a phenomena of earthquakes too.

On one hand I see a decline of true faith, and read '*many false prophets will appear and lead many astray . . . sin will be rampant everywhere and will cool the love of many*' (Matt. 24:11,12 LB). On the other hand I see a tremendous new impetus in evangelism, with the potential of increasing travel possibilities and use of the mass media helping in the completion of Christ's Great Commission. Then I read: '*And the Good News about the Kingdom will be preached throughout the whole world, so that all nations will hear it, and then, finally, the end will come*' (Matt. 24:11 LB).

In the summer of 1968, my travels took me to Czechoslovakia. I walked the bullet-scarred streets of Prague and saw Russian tanks symbolising a war of ideals.

During the summer of 1972, my wife and I drove over the Israeli-occupied Golan Heights and saw relics of the Six Day War during which they were taken. Within weeks after our visit, air space over this area was again filled with the sights and sounds of war.

I saw Vietnam on the television screen, observe tension between India and Pakistan, read of war and massacre in Africa, and then remember that Jesus spoke of 'wars and rumours of wars' preceding the climax of history.

And then I read in J. B. Phillips paraphrases of 2 Timothy 3:1–5, '*You must realize that in the last days the times will be full of danger. Men will become utterly self-centred, greedy for money, full of big words. They will be proud and contemptuous, without any regard for what their parents taught them. They will be utterly lacking in gratitude, purity and normal human affections. They will be men of unscrupulous speech and have no control of themselves. They will be passionate and unprincipled, treacherous, self-willed and conceited, loving all the time what gives them pleasure instead of loving God. They will main-*

tain a facade of 'religion', but their conduct will deny its validity.'

Those observations could be those of a modern journalist, but they were written by the Apostle Paul.

Undoubtedly the most spectacular fulfilment of Bible prophecy is the event most people thought to be impossible. In May 1948, Jews scattered across the face of the earth returned to their historic homeland to establish the modern state of Israel. Newsmen covering the event made hotel reservations for three weeks. In that period they predicted they would cover two big stories – the rebirth of the state of Israel, and its death. A quarter of a century later, little Israel is still defying overwhelming odds against its existence. But God planned the return, had it recorded in His Word, and fulfilled his promise.

Jesus added another detail to prophecy concerning the Jews. '*Jerusalem shall be conquered and tramped down by the Gentiles until the period of Gentile triumph ends in God's good time*' (Luke 21:24 LB).

'God's good time' may well have been in June 1967 when, for the first time since 586 BC, the divided city of Jerusalem was united under Jewish jurisdiction!

Arnold Toynbce, no Biblical prophet, claims: 'By making more and more lethal weapons, and at the same time making the world more and more independent economically, technology has brought mankind to such a degree of distress that we are ripe for the deifying of any Caesar who might succeed in giving the world unity and peace.'

Eminent journalist and Chief Leader Writer of the *Daily Express* James McMillan, in his masterly survey of the erosion of traditional values in Britain during the sixties,* concludes: 'At best, strong men will take over in the West, imposing their will on a placid generation, grown soft and silly on a diet of meretricious rubbish. The strong

*THE ROOTS OF CORRUPTION, published by Tom Stacey. Price£2.00

men will not necessarily be in the Hitler, Mussolini vein. They will simply take the reins of power from corrupt politicians and *tell* people what they have to do.'

The Bible indicates that these and other secular observers who speak of a super-rule are making accurate assessments. In 2 Thessalonians, chapter 2, it describes in detail a coming world ruler. Bible students usually refer to him as the Anti-Christ.

I've no doubt whatever that God is taking the seemingly tangled threads of a world plunging further into darkness and despair, and weaving them according to His eternal and clearly stated plan. And the more I see of world events and trends, the more I feel my days of being a travelling man, as I know them now, are numbered. That's why whatever God gives me to do is tinged with urgency.

For the Christian, there are no dark doubts about the future. My most important trip is already planned. The Bible gives me a number of details about it, but the general picture is drawn by Jesus: '*Let not your heart be troubled. You are trusting in God, now trust in me. There are many homes up there where my father lives, and I am going to prepare them for your coming. When everything is ready, then I will come and get you* . . . ' (John 14:1–3 LB).

The last bit sounds as natural as my wife saying: 'When lunch is ready, I'll call you'. Those words lay the foundation for keen anticipation on my part because I like her cooking! Similarly the promise of Jesus to 'come and get' me causes exciting anticipation.

The cost of the trip will not need to be paid by cash or credit card. Jesus paid it when He died to make it possible. His invitation for this trip extends to all. The miracle at Calvary was not only that Christ died for the sins of the whole world, but that His sacrifice was the result of a deep love and concern for every individual who has been, is or ever will be part of the human race.

All that remains is, by faith, to accept this and make a

personal commitment to Him.

Will the trip on which He takes me be my last? The Bible promises '*things beyond our seeing, things beyond our hearing, things beyond our imagining, all prepared by God for those who love him*' (1 Corinthians 2:9 NEB). So if my finite human thought processes are incapable of comprehending my future home, forgive me if my imagination runs wild for a moment!

One day, about a thousand years from now (although time will cease to be measured by then), my celestial telephone will somehow attract my attention. (It won't ring because I hate the interrupting insistence of that sound!) On the other end of the line will be a friend I once met in some far-flung corner of Europe.

'Hey Dave,' he'll say, 'we're having a special get-together and we want you to come across and join us.'

I'll restrain my automatic reflex action of reaching for my diary to check my bookings. Habits die hard. There will be no diaries then.

'We've got quite a crowd over here,' my friend will continue. 'There's a Portuguese high school student who attended a meeting at which you preached in Evora . . . and then there's an ex-Customs officer who remembers clearing your equipment through Dover . . . and a girl who was introduced to the Lord through one of Cliff Richard's Gospel Concerts in Stockholm. And there's one fellow you must meet . . . says he only met you once before, very briefly, when he was a ticket collector on a train in Eastern Europe . . . and . . . and . . . '

'Sounds great! I can't wait to come,' I'll reply, hanging the receiver in mid-air. (Somehow, to me, gravity seems a very earthly thing!)

And as I take off for yet another great reunion, I will stop and think . . . maybe I do qualify for the title a friend once bestowed on me when I was chasing around the world.

'Foster,' he said, 'you're the *eternal* traveller!'